Ana Merino

Peter Rutherford

Dialogs in Real English

Diálogos en Español Real

Bilingual Parallel Texts
English - Spanish

Second Editio

LANGUAGE TEACHING
ANGLO
DIDACTICA

ANGLO DIDACTICA
PUBLISHING

GW00691932

Impreso en España.
Printed in Spain.
ISBN: 84-95959-00-3
Depósito legal: M-4536-2005

Anglo Didáctica Publishing
C/ Santiago de Compostela, 16
28034 Madrid – Spain.
Tel y fax: +34 91 378 01 88.

Impreso por Fareso, S.A.
Paseo de la Dirección, 5 – 28039 Madrid.

PRESENTATION

This book consists of **20 dialogs**, each presented in both **English and Spanish** and reflecting authentic situations from real life.

In this selection of conversations, the language employed ranges from the colloquial to the more formal, but in every case it is natural and up-to-date. The variety of themes and situations makes it especially useful for comprehension and practice in talking.

Each dialog portrays a scene incorporating a number of elements that can be used to prompt various topics of conversation. In this way, the material provided assists the student, encouraging him to gain confidence in handling modern daily conversation.

The **aim** of this book is multiple. Firstly, it brings the student into touch with the **real language** he is going to hear in an English-speaking country, with the typical expressions used by native speakers, and with words and phrases which, although quite common, are not usually taught in textbooks. By this means the student learns aspects of the day-to-day language that may not have an equivalent in his own but are important to know.

Secondly, for the teacher of English there are varied exercises of comprehension and for conversation practice. The situations can be used, moreover, as short theatrical scenes that serve perfectly for role-play. This kind of material can be found in the section called **Teamwork**.

And lastly, the book can be useful for "**exchange**" lessons, where Spanish-speaking and English-speaking students meet to talk half the time in one language and half in the other. Here they will find plenty of discussion material to fill the period available.

The two pages following each dialog are taken up with these different kinds of **comprehension exercises** and **grammar practice** based on the dialog theme:

1. **True or False?** The student's answers to these questions reveal whether and how well he has understood the text.

2. **What would you say in these situations?** The student has to choose the right phrase out of the three offered.

3. **Text Reconstruction.** The student has to put sentences into a logical order to make sense.

4. **Find the phrase that...** Here the student has to look for exact equivalents in the dialog – a recognition test and a way of learning more.

5. **Grammar Practice.** English grammar is under constant revision throughout, and from a practical standpoint.

Complete answers to all these exercises will be found at the end of the book.

The section on **Teamwork** provides material for active practice, to be performed either under the class teacher's supervision or between the reader and one or more companions. On account of its free nature, no prescribed answers can be given. There are three kinds of exercise here:

1. **Open Questions.** Answer in your own words. This is a series of questions to which the answers must be found in the dialog. If so desired, the teacher (or the student) can easily devise further questions of a similar nature to exploit the material more fully.

2. **Conversation Topics.** Three of these are provided for each dialog theme. The participants are free to expand each topic as they wish and allow it to develop into a full discussion.

3. **Role-play.** This exercise falls into two categories: one that requires a replay of the complete scene, using the original words; and one which introduces certain significant changes that oblige the performers to adapt the dialog accordingly.

The Authors.

PRESENTACION

Este libro ofrece **20 diálogos bilingües inglés-español,** presentados de forma paralela, y que reflejan situaciones de la vida real.

Se trata de una selección de conversaciones cuyo léxico puede tener un registro más coloquial o más formal, siendo, en todo caso, muy fluido y actual. Por la variedad de las situaciones y de los temas tratados, esta obra representa un material de gran utilidad para conversación y comprensión.

Cada diálogo describe una escena en la que se hallan presentes varios elementos que pueden suscitar distintos temas de conversación. De este modo, el libro ayuda e impulsa al estudiante a hablar sobre temas actuales y cotidianos.

El **objetivo** de esta obra es múltiple. Primero, el libro pretende poner al estudiante en contacto con el **idioma real** con que se va a encontrar en un país de habla inglesa, con las expresiones típicas que utiliza la gente y con palabras y frases que, aunque son muy corrientes, no se enseñan normalmente en los libros de texto. El estudiante aprende, de esta manera, vocabulario y expresiones cotidianas, que no siempre tendrán equivalente en su idioma nativo, pero que ha de conocer y aplicar.

Segundo, la obra proporciona al profesor de inglés, variados ejercicios de **conversación y comprensión.** Además, las situaciones propuestas se pueden utilizar como cortas escenas de teatro, para las clases en las que el profesor quiera introducir ejercicios de **Role-play.** En el capítulo de **Teamwork** (Trabajo en equipo) se encuentra este material.

Por último, el libro también puede ser útil en las clases llamadas "**de intercambio,**" en las que estudiantes de habla española se reúnen con estudiantes de habla inglesa para hablar la mitad del tiempo en un idioma y la otra mitad, en el otro. En este libro encontrarán material de conversación y discusión.

Detrás de cada uno de los diálogos, en las dos páginas siguientes, se ofrecen los siguientes tipos de **ejercicios de comprensión** y de **práctica de gramática** basados en el tema tratado:

1. **True or False?** El estudiante demuestra que ha comprendido el texto respondiendo *true* o *false* a cada una de las afirmaciones.

2. **What would you say in these situations?** Se propone una situación y se pide al estudiante que diga lo más apropiado en ese caso, eligiendo la respuesta correcta de entre tres posibilidades.

3. **Reconstrucción del texto.** El estudiante ha de ordenar unos recuadros para construir un diálogo corto que tenga sentido.

4. **Find the phrase that ...** Aquí el estudiante ha de encontrar en el diálogo la frase exacta donde se dice lo mismo que el enunciado. Se trata de un ejercicio de reconocimiento y una forma de ampliar el aprendizaje.

5. **Grammar Practice.** A lo largo de libro se hará un repaso a la gramática inglesa, desde un punto de vista práctico.

Al final de la obra, figuran las respuestas de estos ejercicios.

En el capítulo **Teamwork (Trabajo en equipo)** se ofrece material para la práctica activa, que puede realizarse bajo la supervisión del profesor o entre el lector y uno o más compañeros. Por la naturaleza libre de las respuestas, no se ofrecen soluciones. Hay tres tipos de ejercicios.

1. **Open Questions (Preguntas abiertas).** Responde con tus propias palabras. Se trata de una serie de preguntas, cuyas respuestas se han de buscar en el diálogo. Gracias a la variedad de elementos que componen cada diálogo, le será fácil al profesor o al estudiante idear otras preguntas para la explotación del texto.

2. **Conversation Topics (Temas de conversación).** Se ofrecen tres temas de conversación para cada diálogo, sobre los que los participantes pueden opinar.

3. **Role-play (Escenificación).** Se proponen dos tipos de ejercicios: primero el equipo ha de escenificar el mismo diálogo, usando las mismas palabras; en un segundo momento, los participantes han de representar la escena, introduciendo los cambios que se sugieren y adaptando el diálogo a los mismos.

Los autores.

6

CONTENTS

1. A Chat between Friends after Work. *Charla de dos amigos después del trabajo.* 8
2. At the Insurance Company. *En la compañía aseguradora* 12
3. In the Home. *Asuntos de casa.* 16
4. At a Car Repair Shop. *En el taller del coche.* 20
5. A Telephone Conversation between Two Women. *Conversación de dos amigas por teléfono* 24
6. Management Meeting. *Reunión de directivos* 28
7 Looking for a Flat. *Buscando piso* 32
8 An Evening with Friends. *Una velada con amigos.* 36
9. Looking for an Apartment to Rent. *Buscando un apartamento de alquiler* 40
10. A Conversation between Two Sisters in a Car. *Conversación de dos hermanas en el coche.* 44
11. Shopping. *De compras.* 48
12. A Conversation in the Office. *Conversación en la oficina.* 52
13. At the Bank. *En el banco* 56
14. Picking up a Customer at the Airport. *Al ir a recoger a un cliente al aeropuerto* 60
15. At the Hairdresser's. *En la peluquería* 64
16. Arrival in New York. *Llegada a Nueva York* 68
17. At the Doctor's Office. *En la consulta del médico* 72
18. Having Work Done in the House. *Obreros en casa* 76
19. At a Car Dealer's. *En un concesionario de coches* 80
20. Radio Interview. *Entrevista en la radio* 84

Teamwork. *Trabajo en equipo* 89
Answer Key. *Soluciones a las actividades* 103

1. A CHAT BETWEEN FRIENDS AFTER WORK

Situation: Charlie and Mark have arranged to meet in a bar after work. Mark is already sitting at a table when Charlie arrives.

Charlie:	Hi, Mark. Here I am. Been waiting long?
Mark:	Not too long. Less than ten minutes, I reckon. What'll you have? A beer?
Charlie:	Fine, and a cheeseburger, I think.
Waitress:	Are you ready to order now, sir?
Mark:	Yes, two cheeseburgers and two beers, please.
Waitress:	Two cheese, two beers. Thank you.
Mark:	Well, Charlie, what's new? How's the job going?
Charlie:	I'm getting on pretty well now. I wasn't too happy at first, you remember, but now I've been given a special project to work on, and it's coming along nicely. How about you?
Mark:	No change workwise, but I have news for you: we've bought a small house in the country, with a large yard full of fruit trees.
Charlie:	You don't say! That's great! Whereabouts is it?
Mark:	Not at all that far, actually. The nearest village is a place called Woodlake.
Charlie:	Oh, I know Woodlake. We drove through it a week or two ago. Charming little place, I thought. How far is your new house from there, Mark?
Mark:	Only two miles to the west. So we're near enough for day-to-day shopping, you see, but not actually *in* the village.
Charlie:	Tell me more. Are you planning to move there?
Waitress:	*(Brings their order).* Here you are, gentlemen.
Mark:	Thank you. *(To Charlie).* Cheers!
Charlie:	Cheers!
Mark:	Did you say move there? Oh, no. It's rather small, as I said – only two bedrooms, but it's ample for weekends.
Charlie:	Well, good for you! When can we come and see it?
Mark:	I was thinking of this coming Saturday – how about that?
Charlie:	Yes, I should think that'll be ideal. But I'll check up with Susan this evening and give you a call... Oh, and you can just put that wallet back; *I'm* paying for this!
Mark:	*(Chuckling).* OK, OK! I'll let you treat me this time. You deserve it for keeping me waiting!

1. CHARLA DE DOS AMIGOS DESPUES DEL TRABAJO

Situación: Charlie y Mark han quedado para charlar en un bar después del trabajo. Mark está sentado a una mesa cuando llega Charlie.

Charlie: Hola, Mark. Ya estoy aquí. ¿Llevas mucho tiempo esperando?

Mark: No mucho. Como diez minutos. ¿Qué quieres tomar? ¿Cerveza?

Charlie: Sí. Y una hamburguesa con queso.

Camarera: ¿Qué van a pedir los señores?

Mark: Nos trae, por favor, dos hamburguesas con queso y dos cervezas.

Camarera: Dos hamburguesas, y dos cervezas. Enseguida.

Mark: Bueno, Charlie, ¿qué hay? ¿Qué tal te va el trabajo?

Charlie: Ahora me va muy bien. Al principio no estaba contento, como sabes, pero ahora me han encargado un proyecto, que va saliendo bastante bien. ¿Y a ti, qué tal te va?

Mark: De trabajo, igual. Pero tengo una novedad: nos hemos comprado una pequeña casa en el campo, con un terreno grande y árboles frutales.

Charlie: Vaya, ¡qué bien! ¿Dónde está?

Mark: La verdad es que no está tan lejos. El pueblo más cercano se llama Woodlake.

Charlie: Ah, ya. Conozco ese pueblo. Pasamos por allí hace una o dos semanas. Es un pueblo muy bonito. ¿A qué distancia está tu casa del pueblo, Mark?

Mark: Sólo a unas 2 millas hacia el oeste. Así que tenemos el pueblo a mano para la compra diaria, pero no estamos exactamente dentro.

Charlie: ¿Y qué más? ¿Os vais a mudar allí?

Camarera: *(Trae lo que han pedido).* Aquí tienen, señores.

Mark: Gracias. *(A Charlie).* ¡A tu salud!

Charlie: ¡A la tuya!

Mark: ¿Mudarnos? No, ¡que va! La casa es pequeña: sólo tiene dos habitaciones, pero es bastante para los fines de semana.

Charlie: Bien. ¡Me alegro por vosotros! ¿Cuándo nos la vais a enseñar?

Mark: Estaba pensando en este mismo fin de semana. ¿Qué te parece?

Charlie: Muy bien. Lo consultaré con Susan y esta noche te llamo... ¿Qué vas a hacer? Guarda el billetero. Invito yo.

Mark: *(Riéndose).* Está bien. Te dejo que invites esta vez. ¡Al menos, por lo que me has hecho esperar!

ACTIVITIES

1. True or False?

1. In talking about his new home, Mark had no intention of inviting Charlie and Susan to see it.
2. The house that Mark has bought has fruit trees in the yard.
3. Charlie suggests sharing the cost of the snack.
4. Mark's new house is not far from a place called Woodlake.
5. They order cheese with their beer.
6. Mark and his wife don't intend to move into the new house; they only want to use it for weekends.

2. What would you say in these situations?

1. Has quedado con tu amigo Mark en el bar. Entras y le ves. Ha llegado antes que tú. Tal vez lleve mucho tiempo esperando.

   a) Hi, Mark. Here I am. Been waiting long?
   b) Hello, Mark. What are you doing here?
   c) Hi, Mark. I thought we were meeting tomorrow.

2. Inicias una conversación con tu amigo Charlie hablando de su trabajo.

   a) Well, Charlie, what kind of work do you do?
   b) Well, Charlie, what's new? How's the job going?
   c) Charlie, tell me about your new car.

3. Tu amigo se ha comprado una casa en el campo. Te invita a verla, pero le dices que lo quieres consultar primero con tu mujer, Susan, y que luego le llamarás.

   a) Don't bother to invite us. Susan doesn't like the country.
   b) OK. Let's go. Susan will enjoy it.
   c) I'll check up with Susan this evening and give you a call.

ACTIVITIES

3. Find the phrase that...

1. **Emplea** la camarera para tomar nota de lo que van a tomar.
2. **Pregunta** la distancia que hay desde la casa que se ha comprado Mark hasta el pueblo más cercano.
3. **Resume** en qué situación se encuentra Charlie en su trabajo.
4. **Describe** cuántas habitaciones tiene la casa que se ha comprado Mark.
5. **Sugiere** que Mark no tenía idea de que Charlie le fuera a invitar.

4. Grammar Practice

A. After reading the dialog, put the words from these two columns together, matching those in the first column with those in the second.

A SMALL	VILLAGE
A CHEESE	SHOPPING
THE NEAREST	MINUTES
FRUIT	PROJECT
A SPECIAL	TREES
DAY-TO-DAY	HOUSE
TEN	BURGER

B. From the list of particles on the left, choose the correct one to replace the symbol ♦, and then say the complete sentence aloud.

UP	1) I'm getting ♦ pretty well now.
THROUGH	2) The project is coming ♦ nicely.
ON	3) We drove ♦ it a week or two ago.
BACK	4) I'll check it ♦ with Susan this evening.
ALONG	5) You can put that wallet ♦.

2. AT THE INSURANCE COMPANY

Situation: Simon goes to his insurance company's office to report an accident in which his car was involved.

Clerk: Good morning. Can I help you?

Simon: Morning. I've come to report a car accident.

Clerk: Oh, right, sir. Please take a seat. Have you brought your policy?

Simon: Yes, here you are. I'm fully covered.

Clerk: Good, thank you. *(Reading)* Mr Simon Greene. I'll just locate you on the computer and then you can give me the details of the accident. Ah, here we are. Now, what happened?

Simon: Well, I was coming out of Bernard Street and turning left onto Moon Street. A van, which was stopped at the traffic lights in the opposite direction, suddenly started, ran the red light and crashed into my right-hand door.

Clerk: I see. Had the light changed against you, by any chance?

Simon: No, I wasn't the last car to leave Bernard Street, either; there was a car behind me. It was lucky he saw what happened, otherwise he might have run into me too!

Clerk: Right. And I take it you were going fairly slowly. Is that so?

Simon: Of course.

Clerk: Any injuries?

Simon: No, luckily. But there's a big dent in my door.

Clerk: Do you have the other driver's details?

Simon: Yes, here they are.

Clerk: Right. Let's get all the facts on record... Damage to vehicle: large dent in front right-hand door... Anything else?

Simon: No. That's quite correct.

Clerk: *(Taking the printed sheet from the machine).* Sign here, Mr Greene, will you? ... Thank you. This is your copy. All you have to do now is take it to any of the workshops that do repairs for us. Have you got a list of them?

Simon: Yes, I was given one when I took the insurance out, thanks.

Clerk: You're very welcome.

Simon: Goodbye.

Clerk: Goodbye, sir.

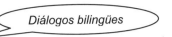

2. EN LA COMPAÑÍA ASEGURADORA

Situación: Simon acude a su compañía aseguradora a dar parte de un accidente que ha tenido con el coche.

Empleado:	Buenos días. Usted me dirá.
Simon:	Buenos días. Vengo a dar un parte de accidente.
Empleado:	Muy bien. Tome asiento. ¿Ha traído la póliza?
Simon:	Sí, tenga. El coche está a todo riesgo.
Empleado:	Muy bien. Gracias. *(Leyendo)* Mr Simon Greene. Ahora mismo le busco en el ordenador y me dice usted los detalles del accidente. Ah, ya está. Dígame cómo fue.
Simon:	Vamos a ver. Yo estaba situado en Bernard Street, giro a la izquierda para entrar en Moon Street, y en ese momento, una furgoneta que estaba parada en el semáforo, en dirección opuesta, de repente arranca, se salta el semáforo rojo y me abolla la puerta derecha.
Empleado:	Sí, ya me hago idea. ¿Tenía usted el semáforo en rojo, por casualidad?
Simon:	No. De hecho un coche venía detrás de mí, que afortunadamente, lo vio, pues si no, me habría dado también.
Empleado:	Muy bien. Todo se produjo a escasa velocidad, ¿no?
Simon:	Sí.
Empleado:	¿Heridos?
Simon:	No, afortunadamente. Sólo que tengo una abolladura muy grande en la puerta.
Empleado:	Los datos del contrario, ¿los tiene?
Simon:	Sí, tenga.
Empleado:	Muy bien. Vamos a tomar nota de todo... Daños en el vehículo: abolladura en puerta lateral derecha. ¿Algo más?
Simon:	No. Está bien así.
Empleado:	*(Saca el impreso por la máquina).* Firme aquí, Mr Greene, por favor... Gracias. Tenga, esta es la copia. Ya puede ir a uno de nuestros talleres concertados. ¿Tiene la lista?
Simon:	Sí, me la dieron cuando hice la póliza, gracias.
Empleado:	No hay de qué.
Simon:	Adiós.
Empleado:	Adiós, señor.

ACTIVITIES

1. True or False?

1. Simon's car was hit by the one behind him.
2. Simon cannot produce his policy.
3. A van started up before the light had changed.
4. Simon's car has a dent in the right-hand door.
5. Two people, Simon and the van driver, were both injured.
6. The clerk believes that Simon jumped the red light.

2. Text Reconstruction
Put these sentences into a logical order.

1	Yes, here you are. I'm fully covered.

2	Oh, right, sir. Please take a seat. Have you brought your policy?

3	Good morning. I've come to report a car accident.

4	Good, thank you. Well, now, what happened?

5	Well, I was coming out of Bernard Street and turning left onto Moon Street. A van, which was stopped at the traffic lights on the opposite direction, suddenly started, ran the red light and crashed into my right-hand door.

ACTIVITIES

3. Find the phrase that...

1. **Indica** que la compañía aseguradora correrá con los gastos del arreglo del coche y Simon no tendrá que pagar nada.
2. **Usa** el empleado para preguntar si Simon también se saltó el semáforo rojo.
3. **Describe** cómo fue el accidente.
4. **Presupone** que la velocidad de los coches implicados era muy lenta.
5. **Da instrucciones** sobre lo que Simon ha de hacer una vez dado el parte.

4. Grammar Practice

Prepositions. After reading the dialog, choose the correct preposition for each sentence from the box, to replace the symbol ◆, and then say the complete sentence aloud.

IN TO FOR ON OF AT INTO
FROM FOR THROUGH

1. I'll just locate you ◆ the computer.
2. Please give me the details ◆ the accident.
3. A van was stopped ◆ the traffic lights.
4. The van crashed ◆ my right-hand door.
5. There's a big dent ◆ my door.
6. Now, take the car ◆ any of the workshops that do repairs ◆ us.
7. We drove ◆ Woodlake a week or two ago.
8. How far is your new house ◆ there?
9. The house is ample ◆ weekends.

3. IN THE HOME

Situation: Rose is at home, waiting to go to work. Mary, her daily help, arrives.

Rose:	Oh, hello, Mary!
Mary:	Morning. How are things?
Rose:	Not too bad, thank you.
Mary:	What d'you want me to do today? Anything special?
Rose:	Well, it's ironing day today. Look, I've set it up for you. Apart from that, just sweep up and mop the floor as usual, please.
Mary:	Right.
Rose:	The kitchen's clean, and don't bother about the windows until it stops raining... But do water the plants if you have time, will you?
Mary:	OK.
Rose:	Oh, and while I think of it, could you slip out and get me some bread this morning? We're right out.
Mary:	It's the wrapped sliced white loaf that you use, isn't it?
Rose:	That's the kind. There's some small change in the Chinese pot on the mantelpiece. Well, now I really must be off to work. *(Puts her coat on)*. Uh-oh, how forgetful of me! I nearly forgot: the plumber's coming later on. The bathroom sink is stopped up. I called him and he said he'd be coming this morning but he couldn't say exactly when.
Mary:	Don't worry. I've only got to go out for the bread. After that I'll be in all morning.
Rose:	I've left the money for the plumber on the kitchen table. If anyone calls, take the message, will you, and get the number so that I can call back. Bye, then.
Mary:	Right. I'll do that. Bye.
	(Later that morning the doorbell rings. It's the plumber).
Mary:	*(Opening the door)*. Are you the plumber?
Plumber:	Yes, ma'am.
Mary:	Come in, please. It's this way. It's the sink here; it's clogged, you see.
Plumber:	Uh-huh. Let's have a look. *(Sets to work)*.
Mary:	If you need anything, I'm in the kitchen.
Plumber:	OK.

3. ASUNTOS DE CASA

Situación: Rose está en la casa esperando a ir a trabajar. Llega Mary, la empleada de hogar.

Rose:	¡Hola, Mary!
Mary:	Buenos días. ¿Qué tal?
Rose:	Ya ves. Como siempre.
Mary:	¿Qué quiere que haga hoy? ¿Algo especial?
Rose:	Hoy toca la plancha. Te lo he puesto todo aquí, mira. También, barres la casa y pasas la fregona, como todos los días.
Mary:	Vale.
Rose:	La cocina está limpia. Y no te preocupes por los cristales hasta que no deje de llover... Y riega las plantas, si te da tiempo, por favor.
Mary:	De acuerdo.
Rose:	Ah, espera... ¿puedes bajar a por el pan esta mañana? No nos queda nada.
Mary:	Se refiere al pan blanco de molde que usa usted, ¿no?
Rose:	Sí, ése es. Hay dinero suelto en el jarrón chino de encima de la chimenea. Bueno, me tengo que ir a trabajar ya mismo. *(Se pone el abrigo)* ¡Ay! ¡Qué cabeza la mía! ¡Por poco se me olvida! Va a venir el fontanero. El lavabo del baño está atascado. Ya hablé con él por teléfono, y me dijo que vendría esta mañana, aunque no sabía exactamente a qué hora.
Mary:	No se preocupe. Sólo voy a salir a por el pan, y después no me voy a mover de casa en toda la mañana.
Rose:	Te dejo el dinero para pagar al fontanero encima de la mesa de la cocina. Si llama alguien por teléfono, coges el recado, por favor, y le pides su número para llamarle luego yo después. Adiós.
Mary:	Muy bien. Así lo haré. Adiós.
	(Más tarde suena el timbre de la puerta. Es el fontanero).
Mary:	*(Abre la puerta).* ¿Es usted el fontanero?
Fontanero:	Sí, señora.
Mary:	Adelante. Pase, por favor. Venga por aquí. Se trata del lavabo. Está atascado, como ve.
Fontanero:	Ah, ya... Vamos a echar una ojeada. *(Empieza a trabajar).*
Mary:	Si necesita algo, estoy en la cocina.
Fontanero:	De acuerdo.

ACTIVITIES

1. True or False?

1. Rose doesn't want Mary to clean the windows while it's still raining.
2. Besides ironing, Mary is to sweep up and mop the floor.
3. Rose has called the plumber in because the bathroom sink is clogged.
4. Rose tells Mary she is kind to buy bread for her.
5. On the point of leaving, Mary remembers something very important.
6. Before going, Rose leaves the money for paying the plumber in the kitchen.

2. What would you say in these situations?

1. Se ha acabado el pan. Le dices a tu empleada de hogar que haga el favor de ir a comprarlo esa mañana.

   a) Are you used to eating bread with your meals? If so, buy some, please.
   b) We're out of bread. Please get some, if you have time tomorrow.
   c) Could you slip out and get me some bread this morning? We're right out.

2. A punto de marcharte, acabas de recordar algo importante: el fontanero va a venir esta tarde. ¿Cómo se lo dices a tu interlocutor?

   a) What do you think the plumber is going to do this evening?
   b) Uh-oh, how forgetful of me! I nearly forgot: the plumber's coming later on.
   c) I'm sure I'm not forgetting anything.

3. Te tienes que ir a trabajar y se va haciendo tarde. ¿Qué le dices a la persona que está contigo en ese momento?

   a) I'm sorry you have to leave now.
   b) I really must be off to work.
   c) It's not so late. I'll water the plants before going to work.

ACTIVITIES

3. Find the phrase that ...

1. **Dice** qué tareas hace todos los días la empleada de hogar.
2. **Expresa** dónde guarda Rose un poco de dinero.
3. **Da instrucciones** para el caso de que alguien llame por teléfono.
4. **Indica** la prisa de Rose porque se le hace tarde para ir al trabajo.
5. **Usa** Mary para explicar el problema del lavabo al fontanero mientras le dirige por la casa.

4. Grammar Practice.

A. *This dialog contains a number of verbs in the imperative form. Match the imperatives on the left with a suitable phrase on the right.*

1. Mop	a) the plants if you have time, will you?
2. Don't bother	b) the floor.
3. Do water	c) about the windows.
4. Take	d) the number so that I can call back.
5. Get	e) the message.
6. Come	f) have a look.
7. Let's	g) in, please.

B. *It's normal to contract verbs in spoken English. But what would be the uncontracted forms of the following contractions taken from the dialog?*

1. What **d'you** want me to do today?
2. **It's** ironing day today.
3. **Don't** bother about the windows.
4. **We're** right out.
5. He said **he'd** be coming this morning.
6. **I've** only got to go out for the bread.
7. After that **I'll** be in all morning.
8. If you need anything, **I'm** in the kitchen.

4. AT A CAR REPAIR SHOP

Situation: Michael takes his car to a repair shop for a check-up.

Michael: Morning.

Mechanic: Morning, sir. Is there something I can do for you?

Michael: Yes, I'd like you to give this car a thorough check-up.

Mechanic: A check-up, eh? Well, we have a special offer all this month, if you are interested *(Shows Michael a leaflet)*. Look: change of oil... battery... tires... All that, and this is what we charge. It's well worth it. Oh, yes, *and* a car wash thrown in.

Michael: *(Looking through the leaflet)* H'm. It sounds really good. How come you offer a car wash free?

Mechanic: We're doing this for the whole of January. Each check-up this month includes a wash, inside and outside.

Michael: It's certainly very good value. How long would it take, though? I need it for work, so I can't afford to leave it too long.

Mechanic: I see. We're pretty busy at present... What's the time now? ... Well, I could have it ready for tomorrow morning. How about that?

Michael: OK. ... Oh, no! I've got to be at the airport at ten to pick someone up. It wouldn't give me time enough.

Mechanic: Hold on, sir. Well, let's see... We'll do our very best to have it ready by this evening. Even if the shop looks closed, it won't be; we're always here for a couple of hours after closing time. I'll come and open up for you and you can come in and fetch it.

Michael: Thanks so much. What about payment? Shall I settle up now or when I come for the car?

Mechanic: Now, if you don't mind, sir. You'll find the cashier over there, on the right. Just tell her what make of car it is, the model, and the registration number and so on. Are the keys in the car?

Michael: Yes, I left them in. Well, thank you. See you later, then. Goodbye.

Mechanic: Goodbye, sir.

4. EN EL TALLER DEL COCHE

Situación: Michael lleva el coche al taller para una revisión.

Michael: Buenos días.

Mecánico: Buenos días, señor. ¿Qué puedo hacer por usted?

Michael: Quiero que le hagan al coche una revisión completa.

Mecánico: ¿Una revisión? Bien, tenemos una oferta especial todo este mes, si le interesa *(Le enseña un folleto)*. Mire: cambio de aceite... batería... estado de los neumáticos... Todo, y este es el precio. Es una buena oferta. ¡Ah! Y lavado de coche, incluido.

Michael: *(Hojeando el folleto)* H'm. Está bien. ¿Cómo es que lavan el coche gratis?

Mecánico: Es una promoción. Durante todo el mes de enero, en cada revisión entra el lavado del coche por dentro y por fuera.

Michael: Eso está muy bien... ¿En cuánto tiempo lo tendría? Lo necesito para trabajar, así que no puedo dejarlo mucho tiempo.

Mecánico: Ya le entiendo. Ahora tenemos mucho trabajo... A ver qué hora es... Podría estar listo para mañana por la mañana. ¿Qué le parece?

Michael: De acuerdo... Ah, ¡no! Mañana a las diez he de ir a recoger a una persona al aeropuerto. No me da tiempo.

Mecánico: Un momento, señor. Veamos... Se lo procuraremos tener para esta tarde a última hora. Aunque estemos cerrados, siempre nos quedamos un poco más. Yo le abro en un momento y puede pasar a recogerlo.

Michael: Se lo agradezco de verdad. ¿Cuándo lo abono? ¿Ahora o cuando venga a recoger el coche?

Mecánico: Ahora, si no le importa. Pase por caja, que está allí, al fondo, a la derecha. Le da los datos del coche a la señorita: marca, modelo, matrícula... ¿Tiene el coche las llaves puestas?

Michael: Sí. Las dejé puestas. Bueno, pues, gracias. Hasta luego, entonces. Adiós.

Mecánico: Adiós, señor.

ACTIVITIES

---

1. True or False?

1. Michael wants to do a check-up on his car in the repair shop.
2. The repair shop offers a free car wash throughout January.
3. Michael has read about the special offer in the newspaper.
4. Michael cannot leave his car long because he uses it for work.
5. Michael has to collect someone at the airport tomorrow.
6. The mechanic asks Michael to pay the cashier.

2. Text Reconstruction
Put these sentences into a logical order:

1	Now, if you don't mind, sir. You'll find the cashier over there, on the right. Just tell her what make of car it is, the model, and the registration number and so on. Are the keys in the car?

2	We'll do our very best to have it ready by this evening.

3	Yes, I left them in. Well, thank you. See you later, then. Goodbye.

4	Thanks so much. What about payment? Shall I settle up now or when I come for the car?

5	Goodbye, sir.

ACTIVITIES

3. Find the phrase that...

1. **Describe** lo que Michael quiere que le hagan al coche.
2. **Indica** en qué consiste la oferta y cuánto tiempo la tendrán.
3. **Explica** por qué Michael necesita el coche mañana por la mañana.
4. **Pregunta** cuándo se abona el servicio.
5. **Usa** el mecánico para saber dónde están las llaves del coche.

4. Grammar Practice

A. Modal Verbs. Choose the correct Modal Verb for each sentence. Some examples belong to earlier dialogs.

1. Is there something I can / may do for you?
2. How long shall / would it take?
3. I won't / can't afford to leave it too long.
4. What about payment? Shall / Will I settle up now or when I come for the car?
5. Could / Should you slip out and get me some bread this morning?

B. Conjunctions. Of the five conjunctions in the box (some of which belong to earlier dialogs) choose the correct one to replace the symbol ♦, and then say the complete sentence aloud.

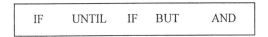

| IF | UNTIL | IF | BUT | AND |

1. We have a special offer all this month, ♦ you are interested.
2. When can we come ♦ see it?
3. Don't bother about the windows ♦ it stops raining.
4. Do water the plants ♦ you have time, will you?
5. I wasn't too happy at first, ♦ now I've been given a special project to work on.

5. A TELEPHONE CONVERSATION BETWEEN TWO WOMEN

Situation: Rose calls her friend, Shirley, to ask her a favor. The phone is answered by a man.

Man:	Hello.
Rose:	Hello. Is Shirley in, please?
Man:	Who's calling, please?
Rose:	This is Rose. I'm a friend of hers.
Man:	Right! Hold on a moment, will you? I'll just call her.
Shirley:	Hello. Who is it, please?
Rose:	It's Rose, dear.
Shirley:	Oh, hello, Rose. Geoffrey didn't tell me who was calling.
Rose:	So it was your husband. I didn't know who it was at first. Listen, I'm calling to ask a favor of you. You don't happen to have Lucy's fancy dress costume – the one she wore last year – do you? I need a costume for Laura, for the school party; it doesn't matter what sort of costume it is.
Shirley:	Well, yes, I've still got it. It's a Cinderella costume, but what I don't have is the hair ribbon and the shoes.
Rose:	Oh, that's great! Don't worry about the ribbon and the shoes; I can make her a nice ribbon with a bit of light blue velvet, and ordinary white shoes will do. They won't be visible anyway. And she'll be wearing woolen stockings, in any case. You know how cold it is in the school theater!
Shirley:	It certainly is! Last year I had to make Lucy wear woolen stockings too, but they were red ones.
Rose:	*(Laughing).* Red stockings under her costume? They would show through!
Shirley:	*(Chuckling too).* No, they did at first, but I made her wear several petticoats over them, and in the end the dress looked very cute. Really something! Oh, by the way, if I were you, I'd take your video camera and film it all. It's well worth filming. I thought it was superb last time.
Rose:	Yes, I was thinking of doing that, you know. Well, how can we arrange it? Shall I come round for it – at about eight, say?
Shirley:	Fine, come at eight, and in the meanwhile, I'll be looking it out.
Rose:	Good. See you then, Shirley. Bye.
Shirley:	Bye.

5. CONVERSACION DE DOS AMIGAS POR TELEFONO

Situación: Rose llama por teléfono a su amiga Shirley para pedirle un favor. Contesta un hombre.

Hombre:	Dígame.
Rose:	Hola. ¿Está Shirley, por favor?
Hombre:	¿De parte de quién?
Rose:	Soy Rose, una amiga suya.
Hombre:	Espere un momento, por favor. Voy a llamarla.
Shirley:	Hola. ¿Quién es?
Rose:	Soy Rose.
Shirley:	Hola, Rose. Geoffrey no me ha dicho quién era.
Rose:	Así que era tu marido. No sabía quién era. Mira, te llamaba para pedirte un favor. ¿No tendrás por casualidad el disfraz de Lucy, el que llevó el año pasado? Es para Laura, para la fiesta del colegio; me da igual de lo que sea. ·
Shirley:	Sí, todavía lo tengo. Es el de Cenicienta, pero le falta la cinta del pelo y los zapatos.
Rose:	¡Ah! ¡Qué bien! No te preocupes por la cinta y los zapatos. La cinta se la hago yo con un poco de terciopelo azul clarito, y los zapatos, unos blancos normales. Total, no se le van a ver. Además, le voy a poner medias de lana de todas formas. ¡Ya sabes el frío que hace en el teatro del colegio!
Shirley:	¡Y tanto! También tuve que ponerle yo a Lucy el año pasado medias de lana, pero eran rojas.
Rose:	*(Riéndose)* ¿Medias rojas debajo del disfraz? ¡Se le clarearían!
Shirley:	*(Riéndose)* ¡Que va! Al principio sí se clareaban; entonces le puse varias enaguas, y, al final, ¡el vestido le quedaba monísimo!... A propósito, te aconsejo que te lleves la cámara de vídeo para grabar la función. ¡Merece la pena grabarla! Me gustó realmente mucho.
Rose:	Sí, la verdad es que ya lo había pensado. Entonces, ¿qué te parece que hagamos? ¿Me paso luego por tu casa a buscarlo, digamos a las 8?
Shirley:	Vale, a las 8 te vienes. Mientras, te lo busco.
Rose:	Bueno. Pues hasta luego, entonces, Shirley. Adiós.
Shirley:	Adiós.

ACTIVITIES

---

1. True or False?

1. Rose calls her friend Shirley for a gossip.
2. It was so cold in the school theater last time that Shirley's daughter had to wear woolen stockings.
3. Last year's show was not a success.
4. Rose will buy a light blue ribbon and white shoes for her daughter's costume.
5. The costume Shirley is going to lend Rose is complete except for a hair ribbon and shoes.
6. The two women arrange to meet the next day.

2. What would you say in these situations?

1. Llaman al teléfono, pero no es para ti, sino para otra persona que está en ese momento en la casa contigo. Quieres saber quién llama para pasarle el recado.

   a) Who's calling, please?
   b) Oh, it's you again. Please don't bother me any more!
   c) That person does not live here.

2. Acabas de pedir a tu amigo que te preste un libro. Quieres ponerte de acuerdo con él y pasar a recogerlo a las ocho.

   a) So, you must have the book ready at eight.
   b) Well, how can we arrange it? Shall I come round for the book – at about nine, say?
   c) Well, how can we arrange it? Shall I come round for it – at about eight, say?

3. Has quedado con tu amigo Robert para las ocho de ese mismo día. Te despides. ¿Qué dices?

   a) Good night.
   b) See you then, Robert. Bye.
   c) We'll meet if you want to.

ACTIVITIES

Find the phrase that...

1. **Dice** de qué es el disfraz que Shirley le presta a Rose.
2. **Indica** por qué el disfraz está incompleto.
3. **Explica** por qué ambas madres quieren poner a sus hijas medias de lana debajo del disfraz de la fiesta del colegio.
4. **Dice** qué idea tuvo Shirley para que las medias rojas no se le clarearan a Lucy debajo del vestido.
5. **Resume** lo mucho que le gustó a Shirley la función del año pasado.

Grammar Practice

A. *Prepositions. In the following sentences from the dialog, the prepositions are missing. Find the correct ones from the box to replace the symbol ✦, and then say the complete sentences aloud.*

AT FOR IN OF ABOUT

1. I didn't know who it was ✦ first.
2. I'm calling to ask a favor ✦ you.
3. I need a costume ✦ Laura.
4. Don't worry ✦ the ribbon and the shoes.
5. You know how cold it is ✦ the school theater.

B. *Adverbs. The dialog contains several very common adverbs, given here. Find the correct ones from the box to replace the symbol ✦, and then say the complete sentences aloud.*

VERY ANYWAY CERTAINLY JUST THEN

1. I'll ✦ call her.
2. See you ✦ , Shirley. Bye.
3. They won't be visible ✦.
4. It ✦ is!
5. In the end the dress looked ✦ cute.

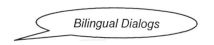

6. MANAGEMENT MEETING

Situation: Robert, Douglas, Andrew and Judy are managers of the same company. Robert is in charge of finance; Andrew handles production; Douglas looks after sales; and Judy is personnel manager.

Douglas: I'm very optimistic about this product we have in mind. Considering its characteristics and market conditions presently, I reckon we could get up to as much as 20% of the market, meaning a sale of 100,000 articles. But to reach that figure and maintain it we will have to hire two more salespeople – and we'll need to be sure of a regular production supply.

Andrew: That's all very well, but there's something important to bear in mind: that we can't just start manufacturing a run of 100,000 units. The articles will have to be run off as they sell. So I'd need an estimate of monthly sales, Doug. And also over a whole year.

Douglas: OK. As soon as I can I'll let you have a sales estimate.

Judy: Doug, you say you need two more salespeople. Well, to allow me to work out how long that'll take, you'll have to tell me exactly *when* you need them and what qualifications you want them to have.

Douglas: I'll do that. But I can tell you this much now: they'll need to be working with us two months before the product goes on the market if we're to have time enough to get them trained.

Judy: Two months, eh? Let me check the calendar... That means I'll have to start the interviewing in January, doesn't it?

Robert: And what about...?

Douglas: *(Interrupting).* Hold on, Bob. Judy, I've checked that up, too, and you're dead right. They would have to begin work in February, so that we could launch the product in April.

Robert: Well, now, may I say something? You all seem to be assuming we're going ahead with this, but we haven't so much as mentioned the overall launching costs. So before we can even plan the production and so on, I must ask each of you to send me a departmental budget, giving me the following: the cost of the raw materials, the ongoing production costs, the salaries of these new employees, and the marketing bill and the trading expenses that all this will entail. Can I count on receiving those first?

The others: Yes... OK... Right.

Diálogos bilingües

6. REUNION DE DIRECTIVOS

Situación: Robert, Douglas, Andrew y Judy son directivos en la misma empresa. Robert es el director financiero. Andrew es el director de producción. Douglas es el director comercial. Judy es directora de recursos humanos.

Douglas: Yo tengo muy buenas expectativas sobre este producto. Según sus características y la situación actual del mercado, estimo que podríamos alcanzar una cuota de mercado del 20%, lo que significaría una venta para el próximo año de 100.000 unidades. Pero para alcanzar esta cifra y mantenerla, necesitaremos dos vendedores más, y el suministro de producto asegurado.

Andrew: Bueno, pero hay una cuestión importante: que no se puede empezar a fabricar 100.000 unidades de una vez. Hay que ir fabricando según se vaya vendiendo. Así que necesitaría un estimado de ventas por meses, Doug. Y por todo el año.

Douglas: Está bien. En cuanto pueda, te paso un estimado de ventas.

Judy: Doug, hablas de que necesitas dos vendedores más. Para calcular el tiempo, me tienes que decir exactamente para cuándo los quieres, y qué perfil profesional han de tener.

Douglas: Lo haré. Pero te digo una cosa: han de incorporarse dos meses antes del lanzamiento del producto, si queremos tener tiempo suficiente para entrenarles.

Judy: Dos meses... ¿eh? Voy a consultar el calendario... Eso significa que tengo que empezar las entrevistas en enero, ¿verdad?

Robert: ¿Y qué hay de...?

Douglas: *(Interrumpiendo).* Espera, Bob, perdona. Judy, yo también he consultado mi agenda, y tienes toda la razón. Se incorporarían a trabajar en febrero, y el lanzamiento del producto sería en abril.

Robert: Bueno, ahora, ¿me dejáis decir algo? Parece que todos suponéis que vamos a seguir adelante con esto, pero aún no hemos hablado de los costes que conlleva el lanzamiento del producto. De modo que antes de planear siquiera la producción, rogaría a cada uno de vosotros que me pasase un presupuesto, de vuestros diferentes departamentos, con lo siguiente: el coste de materias primas, gastos fijos de producción, sueldos de los nuevos empleados, y gastos de comercialización y marketing. ¿Os parece?

Los otros: Estamos de acuerdo. Nos parece bien.

ACTIVITIES

1. True or False?

1. Douglas says that the new product would obtain a 20% share of the market.
2. Judy says she will have to fire two people from their staff.
3. Andrew says they cannot manufacture 100,000 units.
4. The two new employees will have to be trained before they can begin working.
5. It is the training period that determines when to start looking for the new workers.
6. Robert needs to work out the costs before they can launch the new product.

2. Text Reconstruction
Put these passages into a logical order:

| 1 | Doug, you say you need two more salespeople. Well, to allow me to work out how long that'll take, you'll have to tell me exactly when you need them and what qualifications you want them to have. |

| 2 | Yes, you're dead right. They would have to begin work in February, so that we could launch the product in April. |

| 3 | I'll do that. But I can tell you this much now: they'll need to be working with us two months before the product goes on the market if we're to have time enough to get them trained. |

| 4 | Two months, eh? Let me check my calendar... That means I'll have to start the interviewing in January, doesn't it? |

ACTIVITIES

---

3. Find the phrase that...

1. **Dice** que el producto se ha de ir fabricando según se vaya vendiendo.
2. **Emplea** Judy para preguntar por las características que han de reunir los nuevos vendedores que se van a contratar.
3. **Indica** qué es lo primero que harían los nuevos vendedores nada más entrar en la empresa.
4. **Habla** de los costes que conlleva el lanzamiento de un producto.
5. **Da idea** de la fecha en la que los nuevos vendedores empezarían a trabajar para la empresa.

4. Grammar Practice

Cloze Test. In the following paragraph from the dialog, certain words have been removed and put into the box. Put them back to replace the symbols ◆, and then say the text aloud.

AS	IMPORTANT	YEAR	WELL	MIND	JUST	TO
	I'D	RUN	THE	OF	ALSO	

That's all very ◆, but there's something ◆ to bear in ◆: that we can't ◆ start manufacturing a ◆ of 100,000 units. ◆ articles will have ◆ be run off ◆ they sell. So ◆ need an estimate ◆ monthly sales. And ◆ over a whole ◆.

7. LOOKING FOR A FLAT

Situation: Beverly wants to buy a flat. She is on the phone to inquire.

Man: Hello.

Beverly: Good afternoon. I'm calling to ask about the flat you're advertising in The Times.

Man: Yes, how can I help you?

Beverly: Well, first, where is it situated exactly?

Man: Do you know where the new university buildings are?

Beverly: Yes.

Man: Right. Well, it forms part of a small housing estate just on the other side – to the north. It's called Garden City.

Beverly: Oh, yes. I think I know where that is. High-rise buildings in red brick – is that right?

Man: That's it. The address is Pine Avenue, and it's number twelve. The flat is on the fifth floor, overlooking the park, not the main road, so the view is a very good one. There are three bedrooms, as the ad states, with kitchen, two bathrooms, a living room and a large balcony.

Beverly: I see. It sounds right for us. ... What about parking? My husband must be able to put his car away safely.

Man: The ad mentions a space in the car park under the building. That goes with the flat.

Beverly: Oh, so it does. H'm, let's see... Oh yes, the price is a bit higher than we can really afford. Is it negotiable, by any chance?

Man: Well, if you're really interested, why don't you come along and see it, both of you, and we can talk it over. I'm sure you'll like the place. I'm only selling it because my office is being transferred elsewhere and I will have to find a new home there, otherwise...

Beverly: Yes, I reckon we could. Would tomorrow be convenient? How about five p.m.?

Man: OK. That'll be all right. Who should I expect?

Beverly: Oh, sorry: it's Mr and Mrs Welles.

Man: Right, Mrs Wells. I'll see you tomorrow at five, then. And – my name is Jenkins.

Beverly: Thank you, Mr Jenkins. Goodbye.

Man: Goodbye.

7. BUSCANDO PISO

Situación: Beverly quiere comprar un piso. Está informándose por teléfono.

Hombre: Dígame.
Beverly: Buenas tardes. Llamo para preguntar por el piso que anuncian en el Times.
Hombre: Sí, dígame lo que quiere saber.
Beverly: Bien, primeramente, ¿dónde está situado con exactitud?
Hombre: ¿Sabe usted dónde están los edificios nuevos de la universidad?
Beverly: Sí.
Hombre: Bien. Pues el piso está en una pequeña urbanización situada justo al otro lado – hacia el norte. Se llama Ciudad Jardín.
Beverly: Ah, sí. Creo que sé dónde es. Son unos bloques altos, de ladrillo rojo, ¿no es eso?
Hombre: Exactamente. La dirección es Avenida del Pino, y el número es el 12. Es el quinto piso, y da al parque de la urbanización, no a la carretera principal, así que la vista es muy buena. Tiene tres habitaciones, como dice el anuncio, cocina, dos baños, salón y un balcón muy grande.
Beverly: Ya veo. En principio nos vendría bien. ... ¿Y el garaje? Mi marido necesita parking para el coche.
Hombre: El anuncio menciona una plaza de aparcamiento bajo el edificio. Eso entra en el piso.
Beverly: Ah, ya... Esto..., veamos... Ah, sí, el precio es un poco alto para nosotros. ¿Sería negociable?
Hombre: Bueno,... si de verdad les interesa, lo mejor es que vengan ustedes a verlo, y podemos hablarlo. Estoy seguro de que les va a gustar. Yo lo vendo porque mi oficina se traslada a otro sitio y tengo que buscar allí otra casa, si no...
Beverly: Sí, creo que podíamos ir. ¿Le parece bien mañana a las cinco?
Hombre: Estupendo. ¿Cómo se llaman ustedes?
Beverly: Ah, sí,... somos los señores Welles.
Hombre: Muy bien, señora Welles. Hasta mañana entonces, a las cinco. Y yo soy Jenkins.
Beverly: Gracias, señor Jenkins. Adiós.
Hombre: Adiós.

ACTIVITIES

1. True or False?

1. The flat consists of four rooms, plus the kitchen and two bathrooms.
2. The flat is very centrally situated.
3. The owner is selling it because he already has another home somewhere else.
4. They arrange for Beverly to see the place at five p.m. tomorrow.
5. If they buy the flat, Beverly's husband will have to find somewhere for his car too.
6. The flat will probably be quiet and very light, because of what it overlooks.

2. What would you say in these situations?

1. En el periódico The Times has visto un anuncio de un piso. Llamas para informarte. Es por la tarde.

   a) Good morning. I'm calling to ask about the flat you're advertising in The Times.
   b) Hello. Are you the owner of the house advertised in the newspaper?
   c) Good afternoon. I'm calling to ask about the flat you're advertising in The Times.

2. Lo primero es preguntar dónde está el piso exactamente.

   a) Could you tell me if the flat is in a good neighborhood?
   b) Well, first, where is it situated exactly?
   c) Well, how close is it to the underground?

3. A ti te viene bien ir a ver el piso mañana a las cinco. ¿Cómo se lo propones a tu interlocutor?

   a) Would tomorrow be convenient? How about five p.m.?
   b) Could you show me the house tomorrow at five a.m.?
   c) I want to see the flat tomorrow at six.

ACTIVITIES

3. Find the phrase that...

1. **Usa** Beverly para indagar si el propietario estaría dispuesto a rebajar el precio del piso.
2. **Utiliza** el propietario para preguntar cómo se llaman Beverly y su marido.
3. **Explica** la razón por la que el piso está en venta.
4. **Dice** que la plaza de garaje está incluida en el precio.
5. **Sugiere** que el piso no será ruidoso.

4. Grammar Practice

A. Interrogative Words. Choose the correct Interrogative Word from the box to replace the symbol ♦, and then say the complete sentence aloud.

> WHAT   WHY   HOW   WHERE   WHO

1. ♦ can I help you?
2. ♦ is it situated exactly?
3. ♦ about parking?
4. ♦ should I expect?
5. ♦ don't you come along and see it?

B. Pronouns and Possessive Adjectives. Choose the correct Pronoun or Possessive Adjective from the box to replace the symbol ♦, and then say the complete sentence aloud. The numbers tell you how often to use some of them.

> HIS   IT   I(2)   YOU   MY(2)   US

1. How can ♦ help ♦?
2. ♦ husband must be able to put ♦ car away safely.
3. ♦ think I know where that is.
4. ♦ sounds right for ♦
5. ♦ name is Jenkins.

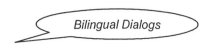

8. AN EVENING WITH FRIENDS

Situation: Ted and Sally have invited some good friends of theirs, another married couple, Alex and Jane, to dinner at their home. Towards the end of the meal, the conversation turns to the theme of unfaithfulness.

Jane: *(Pouring cream over her apple pie)* Ted's a very attractive guy, Sally. Aren't you worried that he might have an affair with one of those sexy young women at his office?

Sally: Me? No way! My husband has too much to do to waste his time on some girl who's only out for promotion! *(Picks up one of the dishes on the table and hands it round).* Anybody fancy more apple pie? Let's finish it up and then we can take the plate away. Jane, what you were saying about affairs... You know, I suspect men often don't know what they're doing in these cases.

Alex: This apple pie is just great! You're really some cook, Sally!

Sally: Thanks, but it was my mother who made it. Does anybody want another Coke?

Jane: Yes, *I* do. Just a drop, please. *(Sally pours some out)* I don't agree, though. Men are not kids; they're fully grown adults and they know quite well what they're doing.

Sally: Or do they? But she – the other woman – she does. Thanks to her, your marriage, your home... it's all at risk, not to mention your bank account. We all know about legal costs! But to my mind maybe one little slip in a marriage lifetime *can* be overlooked – so long as it doesn't happen again!

Alex: *(Bursts out laughing and turns to Ted)* Go on, man! What's to stop you having a smack and tickle now? You know you're gonna be forgiven anyway!

Ted: *(Laughing).* Sure, but I'd only be forgiven for not spending the money!

Alex: So what? *(He picks up the wine and holds it over Ted's glass)* Have some more wine! This is something well worth celebrating! It means there's nothing to hold you back now!

Jane: *(Laughing too)* Alex, don't you go getting ideas! Now pour me out some, too, will you? And some for Sally – she'll need it after hearing your encouragement! *(General laughter).*

8. UNA VELADA CON AMIGOS

Situación: Ted y Sally han invitado a cenar a otro matrimonio, Alex y Jane, unos buenos amigos. Hacia el final de la cena, se produce esta conversación sobre la infidelidad.

Jane:	*(Echándose nata en la tarta de manzana)* Sally, Ted está ahora muy atractivo, ¿no temes que tenga un "affair" con alguna compañera de la oficina?
Sally:	¿Yo? ¡Qué va! Mi marido tiene muchas cosas que hacer y no puede estar perdiendo el tiempo con una chica que sólo quiere promocionarse en la empresa. *(Coge un plato de la mesa y lo pasa).* ¿Alguien quiere más tarta de manzana? Vamos a terminarla y así retiramos el plato de la mesa. Y respecto a lo que tú, Jane, decías de la infidelidad, yo creo que los hombres muchas veces no saben lo que hacen en estos casos.
Alex:	¡La tarta de manzana te ha salido riquísima! ¡Eres una cocinera excelente, Sally!
Sally:	Gracias, pero la ha hecho mi madre. ¿Quién quiere otra coca-cola?
Jane:	Yo. Ponme sólo un poco, por favor. *(Sally se la sirve).* Pues yo no estoy de acuerdo contigo. Los hombres no son niños; son personas adultas, y saben perfectamente lo que hacen.
Sally:	O, a lo mejor, no. En cambio, ella, la otra, sí que pone en peligro tu matrimonio, tu casa,... y tu cuenta bancaria. ¡Que no veas lo que cuesta un abogado! Yo creo que hay casos en que una infidelidad se puede perdonar, con tal de que no se repita otra vez.
Alex:	*(Se echa a reír y dirige a Ted)* ¡Vaya, chico! ¡Qué fácil tienes echar una cana al aire! ¡Te van a perdonar de todas las formas!
Ted:	*(Riéndose)* Sí, pero me van a perdonar, en realidad, por no gastar.
Alex:	¡Y a ti qué más te da! *(Coge el vino y se ofrece para servirlo).* Toma, un poco más de vino. Vamos a celebrar una cosa importante. Y es que en el fondo, y en cierta manera, ¡eres libre!
Jane:	*(Riéndose también).* Alex, no des ideas. Echame vino también a mí, por favor. Y ponle un poco a Sally; ¡lo necesita después de oír cómo animas a su marido! *(Todos ríen).*

ACTIVITIES

1. True or False?

1. Sally comments that her husband is too busy to be interested in promotion at his office.
2. Ted and Sally's guests are a married couple, friends of theirs.
3. Sally says there are cases where unfaithfulness can be pardoned, provided it is not repeated.
4. Jane comes to the conclusion that Ted and Sally are short of money.
5. By the end of the meal both women are drinking wine.
6. Alex proposes a toast.

2. Text Reconstruction
Put these sections into the right order to make sense:

1	Thanks, but it was my mother who made it. Does anybody want another Coke?

2	Or do they? But she – the other woman – she does. Thanks to her, your marriage, your home... it's all at risk, not to mention your bank account. We all know about legal costs!

3	This apple pie is just great! You're really some cook, Sally!

4	Yes, *I* do. Just a drop, please. I don't agree with you, Sally. Men are not kids; they're fully grown adults and they know quite well what they're doing.

5	Have you all heard that? So I'd only be forgiven for not spending the money!

ACTIVITIES

3. Find the phrase that...

1. **Comenta** el alto coste de un proceso de divorcio.
2. **Considera** que hay casos en que una infidelidad se puede perdonar.
3. **Usa** Jane para aceptar el ofrecimiento de Sally de servirle Coca-cola.
4. **Afirma** que Sally es muy buena cocinera.
5. **Propone** un brindis.

4. Grammar Practice

Verb Forms. Say these sentences aloud, with the correct form of verb out of those provided.

1. This is something well worth (celebrate, to celebrate, celebrating)!
2. Not (mention, to mention, mentioning) your bank account.
3. What's to stop you (have, to have, having) a smack and tickle now?
4. It means there's nothing (hold, to hold, holding) you back now!
5. My husband has too much (do, to do, doing) to waste his time on some girl who's only out for promotion.
6. The kitchen's clean, and don't bother about the windows until it stops (rain, to rain, raining).
7. Now I really must be off (work, to work, working).
8. How (come, to come, coming) you offer a car wash free?

9. LOOKING FOR AN APARTMENT TO RENT

Situation: Eddie wants to rent a small apartment in town. He calls a number given in the newspaper.

Woman:	Hello.
Eddie:	Good evening. I'm calling about the apartment you're advertising – the one "close to the town center."
Woman:	Yes. Are you interested in renting it?
Eddie:	Well, it depends... How central is it?
Woman:	How familiar are you with London? The address is in the advertisement: Shaftesbury Avenue, number 1. It couldn't be more central.
Eddie:	I see. How big is it? I mean, what does it consist of?
Woman:	A single bedroom, bathroom, and living room and a "kitchenette." Do you know what that means?
Eddie:	Yes, I've seen them. The kitchen is marked off from the living room by a counter. Is that so?
Woman:	Quite right. And the kitchen is totally electric.
Eddie:	Does the rent include heating and so on?
Woman:	Yes, it's fully inclusive, except for water consumption; you would have to pay for the water you use, of course.
Eddie:	Uh-huh.
Woman:	Forgive my asking, but do you earn a fixed salary? That's one of the tenancy conditions, you see.
Eddie:	Yes. I have some idea of what is required and I know it's necessary to provide some kind of payment guarantee. Well, I hold a State-paid administrative post, so my salary would serve for that.
Woman:	Good. Would you like to see the apartment, then?
Eddie:	Well, maybe. But can we leave it for a day or two? I really need to think it over before committing myself.
Woman:	Very well, but I wouldn't leave it too long if I were you; apartments of this type aren't easy to find, you know.
Eddie:	Yes. Well, I'll call you back soon. Thank you.
Woman:	Goodbye.

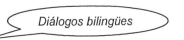

9. BUSCANDO UN APARTAMENTO DE ALQUILER

Situación: Eddie quiere alquilar un pequeño apartamento en el centro de Londres. Llama al teléfono de un anuncio que ve en el periódico.

Mujer:	Dígame.
Eddie:	Buenas tardes. Llamo por el anuncio del alquiler del apartamento... el que dice "céntrico."
Mujer:	Sí. ¿Le interesa alquilarlo?
Eddie:	Bueno, depende... ¿Cómo es de céntrico?
Mujer:	¿Conoce usted Londres? Las señas están en el anuncio: Avenida Shaftesbury, número 1. No puede ser más céntrico.
Eddie:	Ah, ya. ¿Cómo es de grande? Quiero decir... ¿cuántas habitaciones tiene?
Mujer:	Tiene un dormitorio, un baño, un salón, y "cocina americana." ¿Sabe usted a lo que me refiero?
Eddie:	Sí, las he visto. La cocina está comunicada con el salón por un mostrador. ¿Es eso?
Mujer:	Exacto. Y la cocina es totalmente eléctrica.
Eddie:	¿Está incluido en el precio la calefacción, y lo demás?
Mujer:	Efectivamente. Todo está incluido, menos el agua. El consumo de agua correría de su cuenta.
Eddie:	Ah, ya.
Mujer:	Disculpe que le haga esta pregunta. ¿Cuenta usted con una nómina? Es una de las condiciones del contrato, como sabe.
Eddie:	Sí. Tengo idea de lo que se pide. Sé que se necesita una garantía de pago. Yo soy funcionario del Estado... supongo que es bastante.
Mujer:	Muy bien. ¿Desea ver entonces el apartamento?
Eddie:	Tal vez, pero quería pensármelo un par de días, antes de decidirme.
Mujer:	Bien. Pero yo que usted no lo dejaría mucho tiempo, porque estos apartamentos no se encuentran fácilmente.
Eddie:	Bueno, pues la volveré a llamar pronto. Gracias.
Mujer:	Adiós.

ACTIVITIES

1. True or False?

1. The apartment has no guest bedroom.
2. Eddie has no idea what sort of kitchen it is.
3. Eddie would have to pay for the water he uses.
4. He would like to buy the apartment.
5. Eddie offers his salary as rent.
6. Eddie wants time to think it over and promises to call her another time.

2. What would you say in these situations?

1. Crees que tu interlocutor podría no entender una expresión que acabas de decir. Antes de seguir la conversación, quieres asegurarte de que lo comprende. ¿Qué dices?

   a) Do you know what that means?
   b) I don't think you will be able to understand what I mean.
   c) Perhaps you haven't seen such a thing in all your life.

2. Tú eres el propietario. Te interesa saber si el posible inquilino tiene unos ingresos fijos, pues de lo contrario, es inútil enseñarle el apartamento.

   a) Sorry, but do you have a job?
   b) You know that if you don't have a job, it's useless for you to see the apartment.
   c) Forgive my asking, but do you earn a fixed salary?

3. Quieres saber cuántas habitaciones tiene el apartamento. Pregúntaselo al propietario.

   a) Do you like the apartment?
   b) How big is it? I mean, what does it consist of?
   c) Is the apartment big enough for three people?

ACTIVITIES

3. Find the phrase that...

1. **Dice** que todo funciona por electricidad en la cocina.
2. **Afirma** que el apartamento está muy bien comunicado.
3. **Indica** las señas del apartamento.
4. **Describe** lo que se entiende por "cocina americana."
5. **Pregunta** si el precio del alquiler incluye la calefacción.

4. Grammar Practice

A. From affirmative to interrogative. Change these sentences into questions.

AFFIRMATIVE	INTERROGATIVE
1. You are interested in renting it.	...?
2. You know what that means.	...?
3. That is so.	...?
4. The rent includes heating.	...?
5. You earn a fixed salary.	...?
6. You would like to see the apartment.	...?

B. Prepositions. After re-reading the dialog, choose the correct preposition for each sentence from the box to replace the symbol ♦, and then say the complete sentence aloud.

FROM	ABOUT	IN	BY	FOR	OF

1. I'm calling ♦ the apartment you're advertising.
2. The address is ♦ the advertisement.
3. The kitchen is marked off ♦ the living room ♦ a counter.
4. You would have to pay ♦ the water you use.
5. Apartments ♦ this type aren't easy to find.

10. A CONVERSATION BETWEEN TWO SISTERS IN A CAR

Situation: Ann and her sister Betty are going to find a certain store that has been recommended to Ann.

Betty: It's a furniture store, you said, didn't you? Whereabouts is it?

Ann: Just off Commercial Road, they told me. I've got the address here somewhere. Just a minute... Yes, number ten, Wharfedale Street. Do you know where that is?

Betty: No. I only know where Commercial Road is. Well, never mind; jump in and we'll look for it once we're in that area. ... Ann, guess what I heard the other day: Bill and Molly are splitting up!

Ann: You don't say! Bill and Molly? Why?

Betty: She told me that they're always quarreling; but it's been getting worse lately and she can't put up with it any longer. Molly says...

Ann: Oh, turn off at the next corner, on the right – I've just seen a sign for Wellcomes store, and that's on Commercial Road.

Betty: Good. Well, Molly had just about had enough. She told me she's found a lawyer who can handle it for her.

Ann: But what does Bill say about it? Will he agree to a separation?

Betty: Apparently, yes. At least, that's what he says. I wouldn't trust him, you know.

Ann: Well, time will tell. But I do wish they'd gone to a marriage guidance specialist long before it came to this. It might have saved the marriage. Oh, there's Wellcomes, so this must be Commercial Road.

Betty: Yes, it is – there's the street name, on that wall. Look, I'm going to pull up at that service station over there. I'll fill up and we can find out where Wharfedale Street is at the same time.

Ann: Good idea. Tell you what: while you're doing that, I'll go and ask that old gentleman over there. He probably lives in this area. ... Excuse me, but could you direct me to Wharfedale Street?

Man: Yes, it's only two minutes from here. It's at the end of this street. You can't go wrong.

Ann: Thank you very much indeed.

Man: My pleasure.

Ann: *(To her sister)* Get in, Betty. I know where it is now.

10. CONVERSACION DE DOS HERMANAS EN EL COCHE

Situación: Ann y su hermana Betty están buscando una tienda que le han recomendado a Ann.

Betty:	Dijiste que era una tienda de muebles, ¿no? ¿Dónde está?
Ann:	Por Commercial Road, me han dicho. Tengo la dirección en algún sitio. Espera... Sí, Wharfedale número 10. ¿Sabes dónde es?
Betty:	No. Sólo sé por dónde cae Commercial Road. Bueno, no importa, sube al coche y la buscaremos cuando estemos en ese barrio. ... Ann, ¿sabes de lo que me he enterado? ¡Pues que Bill y Molly se separan!
Ann:	¡No me digas! ¿Bill y Molly? ¿Por qué?
Betty:	Ella me ha contado que se pelean continuamente; cada vez es peor y ya no lo aguanta más. Molly dice...
Ann:	Gira a la derecha en la próxima calle. Acabo de ver un cartel de los almacenes Wellcomes, que están en Commercial Road.
Betty:	Bien. Pues Molly me ha dicho que ya estaba harta, y que ha encontrado un abogado que le puede llevar el caso.
Ann:	Pero ¿qué dice Bill de todo ello? ¿Está de acuerdo con el divorcio?
Betty:	Parece que sí. Por lo menos es lo que dice, aunque yo no me fiaría mucho de él.
Ann:	El tiempo lo dirá. Ojalá hubieran ido a un consejero matrimonial mucho antes de llegar a esta situación. Podrían haber salvado el matrimonio. Mira, aquí está Wellcomes, así que ésta tiene que ser Commercial Road.
Betty:	Sí, lo es; lo dice la placa de la calle. Mira, voy a pararme en esa gasolinera. Echo gasolina y, de paso, preguntamos dónde está la calle Wharfedale.
Ann:	Buena idea. Mientras echas gasolina, le preguntaré a ese señor. Probablemente vive por aquí. ... Perdone, ¿sabe usted por dónde cae la calle Wharfedale?
Hombre:	Sí. Tan sólo a unos dos minutos de aquí. Siguiendo esta calle hasta el final; no tiene pérdida.
Ann:	Muchas gracias.
Hombre:	No hay de qué.
Ann:	*(Digiriéndose a Betty).* Vamos, entra en el coche, que ya sé dónde es.

ACTIVITIES

1. True or False?

1. This is a dialog between two people.
2. The store is some way from Commercial Street.
3. Bill and Molly are married.
4. Molly tells them to turn off at the next corner.
5. Bill and Molly are separating because of their constant quarrels.
6. With the directions they are given, they are sure they will find the store.

2. Text Reconstruction
Put these dialog parts into a logical order:

1	Yes, it's only two minutes from here. It's at the end of this street. You can't go wrong.

2	My pleasure.

3	Excuse me, but could you direct me to Wharfedale Street?

4	Thank you very much indeed.

5	Get in, Betty. I know where it is now.

ACTIVITIES

3. Find the phrase that...

1. **Indica** la calle en la que está la tienda que buscan.
2. **Explica** cómo es la relación entre Bill y Molly.
3. **Duda** sobre las intenciones de separación de Bill.
4. **Propone** una solución para salvar el matrimonio de Bill y Molly.
5. **Agradece** la ayuda que les ha dado el caballero de la gasolinera.

4. Grammar Practice

Word Order. Put these isolated words into meaningful sentences. Some of them come from earlier dialogs.

1. do – know – you – that – is? – where

2. I – know – Road – Commercial – is – only – where

3. off – turn – at – next – corner – the

4. what – but – Bill – does – about – say – it

5. I'm – to – up – pull – at – that – station – service – going

6. that – go – and – I'll – ask – gentleman – old – there – over

7. the – calling – you're – I'm – about – advertising – apartment

8. this – something – celebrating! – well – is – worth

11. SHOPPING

Situation: Brian and Rose are in a department store. Brian wants to buy a pair of pants.

Rose: *(To a shop assistant)*. Excuse me. The men's section – which floor is it?

Assistant: On the second floor.

Rose: Thanks. *(To Brian)*. We have to go up to the second floor.

Assistant: *(Seeing them examining some pants)*. Can I help you?

Brian: Yes. These are my size, but I'd like to try them on; they look rather long to me.

Assistant: Don't worry about that, sir. We can always shorten them for you.

Brian: Would it cost much?

Assistant: It's a free service, sir. We don't charge for altering our own articles. If you'd care to try them on, the fitting rooms are at the end there, on the right. When you've got them on, I'll come along and measure them for length. *(Brian takes them and has just put them on when the assistant appears, with Rose a little behind him)*. Now, sir, let's see... They look about right to me. How do you find them? Are they comfortable?

Brian: Yes, they're comfortable enough, but I still think they're a bit too long. *(To Rose)* Rose, what do you think?

Rose: They're very nice, and that's about the right fit. But maybe they could be a little bit shorter.

Assistant: Then we'll take them up for you. *(Produces a box of pins and kneels at Brian's feet)*. I should think that half an inch will do... How about that, sir? Does that look better?

Brian: Oh, yes. That's just right.

Assistant: I'll be outside when you're ready. *(Brian changes back and takes the pants out with him)*.

Brian: When will they be ready?

Assistant: Two or three days, sir. Cash or credit card?

Brian: Cash. Here you are. When shall I collect them, then?

Assistant: On Thursday, sir – any time in the morning. And please don't forget to bring this ticket with you.

Brian: Thank you.

Assistant: Goodbye.

11. DE COMPRAS

Situación: Brian y Rose están en un centro comercial. Brian quiere comprarse unos pantalones.

Rose:	*(Dirigiéndose a una dependienta).* Disculpe. La sección de caballeros, ¿en qué planta está?
Señorita:	En la segunda planta.
Rose:	Gracias. *(Se dirige a Brian).* Tenemos que subir a la segunda planta.
Dependiente:	*(Al ver que están mirando pantalones).* ¿Les puedo ayudar en algo?
Brian:	Sí, estos son de mi talla, pero quería probármelos. Los veo largos.
Dependiente:	Por eso no se preocupe. Se los arreglamos nosotros.
Brian:	¿Cobran algo por el arreglo?
Dependiente:	Es un servicio gratuito, señor. No cobramos el arreglo de nuestros artículos. Si quiere probárselos, los probadores están al fondo a la derecha. En cuanto se los haya puesto, me llama para ajustarle el bajo. *(Brian se los acaba de probar cuando viene el dependiente con Rose, que va detrás).* Aquí estoy, señor. Déjeme ver... Yo se los veo bien. Usted, ¿qué tal se encuentra con ellos? ¿Le resultan cómodos?
Brian:	Sí, son bastante cómodos, pero todavía me parecen un poco largos. *(A Rose)* Rose, ¿tú qué opinas?
Rose:	Están muy bien y son de tu talla. Pero quizás estarían mejor un poquito más cortos.
Dependiente:	Pues entonces, le voy a coger el bajo. *(Saca una caja de alfileres y se agacha).* Con poco más de un centímetro tiene suficiente. ¿Cómo se los ve ahora, señor? ¿Mejor así?
Brian:	Sí. Perfecto.
Dependiente:	Le espero fuera, entonces. *(Brian se cambia de ropa y sale).*
Brian:	¿Cuándo estarán listos?
Dependiente:	En dos o tres días, señor. ¿En efectivo o con tarjeta?
Brian:	En efectivo. Aquí tiene. ¿Entonces, cuándo puedo venir a recogerlos?
Dependiente:	El jueves, a cualquier hora de la mañana. Tenga, no olvide traer este resguardo.
Brian:	Gracias.
Dependiente:	Adiós.

ACTIVITIES

1. True or False?

1. The store assistant offers to show Brian some pants.
2. The pants are too long and need altering.
3. They will be ready on Thursday.
4. Brian will pay for the pants when he calls in for them.
5. The alteration is a matter of shortening the pants half an inch.
6. The store charges for this kind of alteration.

2. What would you say in these situations?

1. Estás en un centro comercial. Quieres ir a la sección de caballeros. Te diriges a una dependienta. ¿Qué dices?

   a) Could you tell me where the elevator is?
   b) Excuse me, where is the women's department?
   c) Excuse me. The men's section – which floor is it?

2. Al ir a pagar, el dependiente te preguntará la forma de pago que prefieres. ¿Qué te dirá?

   a) Cash or credit card?
   b) Are you paying for this?
   c) May I see some identification, please?

3. La tienda se queda con los pantalones que acabas de comprar para ajustarles el bajo. Quieres saber el tiempo que tardan.

   a) How long will I have to wait before my pants are ready?
   b) When will they be ready?
   c) Will you come and pick them up tomorrow?

ACTIVITIES

3. Find the phrase that...

1. **Usa** Brian para decir que quiere probarse los pantalones.
2. **Indica** que la tienda arregla las prendas de forma gratuita.
3. **Utiliza** el dependiente para averiguar la forma de pago que prefiere el cliente.
4. **Dice** el día en que puede Brian pasar a recogerlos.
5. **Recuerda** a Brian que ha de traer el resguardo para recoger la prenda.

4. Grammar Practice

A. After reading the dialog again, choose the correct noun to insert in each sentence, instead of the symbol ◆.

> SERVICE   LENGTH   FLOOR   INCH   TICKET

1. The men's section, which ◆ is it?
2. It's a free ◆, sir.
3. I'll come along and measure them for ◆.
4. I should think that half an ◆ will do.
5. Please don't forget to bring this ◆ with you.

B. Adjectives. Replace the symbol ◆ by a valid adjective from the box.

> COMFORTABLE   SECOND   LONG   READY   RIGHT

1. We have to go up to the ◆ floor.
2. These pants look rather ◆ to me.
3. Are they comfortable? Yes, they are ◆ enough.
4. When will they be ◆ ?
5. Oh, yes. That's just ◆.

12. A CONVERSATION IN THE OFFICE

Situation: Sylvia and Jean are both secretaries working in the same firm. Their immediate boss is Roger and his superior is Arthur.

Sylvia: Hello, Jean! You here already? It's early for you!

Jean: *(Concentrating on her computer)* Hi, Sylvia. Yes, I thought I'd make a special effort today, as I've got to have everything ready for next week's meeting. *(Looks up for the first time).* You're all wet – is it raining?

Sylvia: Pouring! It started the very moment I got off the bus. *(She takes her raincoat off and shakes it well before hanging it up).* Just as well I was wearing this instead of my other coat; this one has a hood. At least it kept my hair dry!

Jean: I only hope it clears up before lunch; I've come without an umbrella... Oh, by the way: this fax came in for you about five minutes ago.

Sylvia: Thanks. Ah, yes. It's the advertising agency's estimate. Goodness! What they charge! I'll put it on Roger's desk. *(She comes back).*

Jean: Oh, I wanted to ask you... How about you and me getting together to talk about the meeting?

Sylvia: Next week's meeting? All right, but what do you want to talk about? It's all arranged, I thought...

Jean: Well, I meant we could discuss how to share the work between us.

Sylvia: Oh, I see. Yes. Fine. Can you manage a few minutes just after lunch, and get some ideas over a coffee?

Jean: OK. Where can we meet?

Sylvia: In the boardroom – at two o'clóck, OK?

Jean: Right. Oh – and another thing: who signs the account for CEEI? You know, the firm that set up our stand at that last congress? I'm asking you because Roger's not here.

Sylvia: Give it to Arthur. When Roger's traveling, he authorizes all that kind of thing. Then file it under "Conventions."

Jean: I see. I'll take it to him right now. I heard him moving about in his office a few minutes ago, so he's in. And that'll be one thing less for me to worry about!

Sylvia: *(Waving an envelope)* Jean! Take this with you, will you? It's Arthur's mail. Thanks a lot.

12. CONVERSACION EN LA OFICINA

Situación: Sylvia y Jean son secretarias en la misma empresa. Su jefe inmediato es Roger, y el superior de éste es Arthur.

Sylvia: Hola, Jean. ¿Ya estás aquí? ¡Qué pronto has llegado hoy!

Jean: *(No levanta la vista del ordenador).* Hola, Sylvia. Sí, es que quería adelantar trabajo porque quiero tener preparado todo para la reunión de la próxima semana. *(Levanta la vista por primera vez).* ¡Estás empapada! ¿Está lloviendo?

Sylvia: ¡Diluviando! Empezó a llover justo al bajar del autobús. *(Se quita la gabardina y la sacude antes de colgarla).* Menos mal que llevaba puesto esto en vez del abrigo; como tiene capucha ¡al menos no me he mojado el pelo!

Jean: Espero que pare antes de la comida. Me he venido sin paraguas... A propósito: ha llegado un fax para ti hace como cinco minutos.

Sylvia: Gracias. Ah, sí. Es el presupuesto de la agencia de publicidad. ¡Qué barbaridad! ¡Qué caro! Lo dejaré en la mesa de Roger. *(Regresa).*

Jean: Ah, quería preguntarte... ¿qué te parece si nos reunimos tú y yo y hablamos sobre la reunión?

Sylvia: ¿La de la próxima semana? Vale, pero de qué quieres hablar. Pensé que ya estaba todo arreglado.

Jean: Bueno, yo quería hablar de cómo nos vamos a repartir el trabajo.

Sylvia: Ya veo. Sí. Buena idea. ¿Te parece que quedemos para después de comer, y hablamos mientras tomamos un café?

Jean: Vale. ¿Dónde quedamos?

Sylvia: En la misma sala de reuniones, como a las dos, ¿te parece?

Jean: Estupendo. Ah, otra cosa... ¿quién firma la factura de CEEI, la empresa que montó el stand en el último congreso? Te lo pregunto porque Roger no está.

Sylvia: Dásela a Arthur. Cuando Roger está de viaje, es él quien autoriza las facturas. Luego la archivas en la carpeta de "Convenciones."

Jean: Sí. Voy a llevársela ahora mismo. Le he oído en su despacho, y así tengo una cosa menos en qué pensar.

Sylvia: *(Agitando un sobre)* ¡Jean! Llévate esto, por favor. Es una carta para Arthur. Muchas gracias.

ACTIVITIES

1. True or False?

1. Sylvia has a higher position in the firm than Arthur.
2. Jean stops work to greet Sylvia.
3. It's raining very hard.
4. Sylvia did not get her hair wet because she was wearing a raincoat with a hood.
5. Roger is away, traveling.
6. Arthur has not yet arrived at the office.

2. Text Reconstruction
Put these boxes into a logical order:

1	In the boardroom – at two o'clock, OK?

2	Oh, I wanted to ask you... How about you and me getting together to talk about next week's meeting? We could discuss how to share the work between us.

3	OK. Where can we meet?

4	Oh, I see. Fine. Can you manage a few minutes just after lunch, and get some ideas over a coffee?

5	Right.

ACTIVITIES

---

3. Find the phrase that...

1. **Afirma** que Jean ha llegado a la oficina mucho antes de su hora.
2. **Indica** el motivo por el que Jean desea que pare de llover.
3. **Propone** una reunión entre las dos secretarias.
4. **Sugiere** que el presupuesto que acaba de pasarles la agencia de publicidad es muy caro.
5. **Describe** qué es lo que ha de hacerse con la factura de CEEI.

4. Grammar Practice

A. Phrasal Verbs. Re-read the dialog and then complete the Phrasal Verbs by finding their missing particles (marked by ◆) in these sentences.

1. She takes her raincoat ◆ and shakes it well before hanging it ◆.
2. I only hope it clears ◆ before lunch.
3. This fax came ◆ for you about five minutes ago.
4. I heard him moving ◆ in his office a few minutes ago, so he's ◆.

B. Verb Forms. Put the verb (indicated in parenthesis) into the correct form to give meaning to each sentence.

1. Is it (rain)?
2. It (start) the very moment I got off the bus.
3. I've (come) without an umbrella.
4. This fax (come) in for you about five minutes ago.
5. What do you (want) to talk about?
6. I'm (ask) you because Roger's not here.
7. I (hear) him moving about in his office a few minutes ago.

13. AT THE BANK

Situation: John has some business to settle at his bank.

John: Morning.

Clerk: Good morning, sir. Can I help you?

John: Yes. I've got one or two matters to deal with. *(Taking a savings book out of his pocket).* First, would you please bring this up to date?

Clerk: Certainly. May I see some identification, please? *(John shows him his driver's license, and the clerk works on the book).* Here you are, sir. Is there anything else?

John: Yes, I want to pay this check into another account I have with you. Where are the forms, please?

Clerk: There are some on the table over there, but take this one. It'll save you time.

John: Thanks. *(He fills the form in and returns it with the check).* There you are. Please check it to make sure I've got it right.

Clerk: Of course... That's quite correct. *(Meanwhile, John looks through the savings book and finds that he has been wrongly charged).*

John: Excuse me, there's a mistake here: a subscription for some golf club has been debited to me. I don't belong to a golf club.

Clerk: Let me have a look, sir, do you mind? I'll check that for you... Yes, you're quite right: I'm afraid it's our mistake. I'll cancel that debit at once. I'm very sorry indeed.

John: Good. Thank you. Now, I want to make a transfer. *(Hands over a piece of paper with written data).* Here are the details, and this is the number of the account the money is to come from.

Clerk: Right. Just a moment. Would you sign here, please? Thank you. This copy is for you. Anything else, sir?

John: Well, yes. I'd like to know a little more about one of the services you offer. Who could inform me?

Clerk: The manager, sir. I don't think he's busy at the moment and I'm sure he'll be only too pleased to help you. Come this way, would you?

13. EN EL BANCO

Situación: John acude a un banco para realizar unas gestiones.

John: Buenos días.
Empleado: Buenos días. ¿Le puedo atender en algo?
John: Sí, gracias. Tengo que hacer varias cosas.... *(Saca una cartilla del bolsillo).* Primero, ¿me podría poner esta cartilla al día?
Empleado: Por supuesto. Déjeme ver su carnet de identidad, por favor. *(John se lo entrega, y el empleado opera con la cartilla).* Aquí tiene, señor, su cartilla. ¿Desea algo más?
John: Sí. Quiero ingresar este cheque en otra cuenta que tengo. ¿Dónde están los impresos de ingreso, por favor?
Empleado: Están sobre aquella mesa, pero tenga, le doy yo uno para que no se moleste usted.
John: Gracias. *(John rellena el impreso, y cuando termina, lo entrega, junto con el cheque, al empleado).* Ya está. Tenga. Por favor, revísemelo para ver si lo tengo bien.
Empleado: No se preocupe... Está todo perfecto. *(Mientras tanto, John revisa la cartilla, y descubre que le han cobrado algo por equivocación).* Disculpe, hay una equivocación en mi cartilla. Me pasan el cargo de un recibo de un club de golf, al que no pertenezco.
Empleado: Déjeme la cartilla de nuevo, por favor. Voy a comprobarlo... Efectivamente se ha producido un error por nuestra parte. Ahora mismo le retrocedo el cargo. Le pedimos disculpas.
John: Gracias. Ahora, quiero hacer una transferencia. *(Le entrega un papel escrito).* Estos son todos los datos,... y éste es el número de mi cuenta de donde quiero que saque el dinero.
Empleado: Muy bien. Pues en un momento... ¿Puede firmar aquí, por favor? Aquí tiene el resguardo. ¿Algo más, señor?
John: Sí. Deseaba información sobre uno de sus productos. ¿Quién me puede informar?
Empleado: El director. Ahora está libre y le atiende enseguida con muchísimo gusto. Pase por aquí, por favor.

ACTIVITIES

1. True or False?

1. There are three people in this dialog.
2. John's golf club has charged him wrongly.
3. He pays a check into one of his accounts with that bank.
4. A mistake has been made, but the clerk corrects it and apologizes.
5. The paying-in-forms are not on display because the clerk hands them out.
6. The bank manager keeps John waiting.

2. What would you say in these situations?

1. Acudes a un banco para hacer varias gestiones. Te interesa ver primero si te han ingresado la nómina en una cartilla que tienes, y para ello, el empleado ha de ponerla al día.

   a) Please check my savings book for me.
   b) I want to know if a withdrawal has been made from my account.
   c) First, would you please bring my savings book up to date?

2. Para operar con tus cuentas, el empleado necesita comprobar tu identidad. ¿Qué te dirá?

   a) I won't do anything unless you identify yourself.
   b) May I see some identification, please?
   c) What is your address and telephone number, please?

3. En algún momento, el empleado puede pedirte que firmes con algún propósito. ¿Qué te dirá probablemente?

   a) You don't need to sign. I will do it on your behalf.
   b) Would you sign here, please?
   c) Sign here. Oh, I don't like your handwriting.

ACTIVITIES

3. Find the phrase that...

1. **Usa** John para informar al empleado de que va a ingresar un cheque y pedir los impresos.
2. **Indica** que el empleado ha entregado a John el justificante de la transferencia.
3. **Utiliza** el empleado para reconocer que el banco ha cometido un error.
4. **Dice** cómo va a solucionar el empleado el error cometido por el banco.
5. **Sugiere** que el director atenderá a John enseguida y con mucho gusto.

4. Grammar Practice

A. Verb Contractions. What are the contracted forms of the phrases shown in **bold letters?**

1. **I am** very sorry indeed.
2. **It will** save you time.
3. **That is** quite correct.
4. **There is** a mistake.
5. **I will** check that for you.
6. **You are** quite right.

B. Prepositions. After reading the dialog, choose the correct preposition for each sentence from the box to replace the symbol ◆, and then say the complete sentence aloud

TO	FOR	ABOUT	AT	INTO

1. I don't think the manager is busy ◆ the moment.
2. I want to pay this check ◆ another account I have with you.
3. I don't belong ◆ a golf club.
4. I'll check that ◆ you.
5. I'd like to know a little more ◆ one of the services you offer.

Bilingual Dialogs

14. PICKING UP A CUSTOMER AT THE AIRPORT

Situation: Judy has been sent by her company to the airport to pick up a very important customer, Monsieur Moreau, who is arriving on the Paris flight.

Judy: Monsieur Moreau? Very pleased to meet you. I'm Judy Gardner, of CEEI. I've come to take you to the office.

Moreau: Oh, how do you do? It's very kind of you to pick me up.

Judy: Do you have all your baggage with you?

Moreau: Yes, all I have is this little case.

Judy: Then let's go. I have a car parked just outside. How was the flight, Monsieur Moreau?

Moreau: Very good, I'm glad to say. ... Excuse me, did you say your name was Garland?

Judy: *(Laughing)* Oh, no – Gardner. It's not the first time I've been confused with somebody famous! It's Gardner, and my first name's Judy. I work for Mr Steinbeck.

Moreau: Oh, I see. *(They get in the car).*

Judy: This is your first visit here, I was told. Is that so?

Moreau: Quiet right. I've been three or four times to Toronto, but I've never had occasion to come here before. And it's a great pity, because I understand there's a lot to see.

Judy: Well, business trips are like that, aren't they? It's all go, go, go, and no time for yourself.

Moreau: Actually, my daughter asked me to get her a CD that's just come out – a collection of songs by The Beatles – but I know I'll go back empty-handed.

Judy: Well, I don't know... It's only three o'clock and your meeting doesn't start until five. Would you like to stop and look for it? There's a big store right on our way into town.

Moreau: Would there really be time? I'd be most grateful to you, Miss Garland – I mean Gardner.

Judy: Sure. No problem. Besides, there's very little traffic at this time of day.

Moreau: It's very good of you: my daughter will be so pleased.

Judy: But this is something we can only do at three p.m. Later, it would be just impossible – the traffic's much too heavy.

Moreau: That sounds exactly like Paris, you know!

14. AL IR A RECOGER A UN CLIENTE AL AEROPUERTO

Situación: La compañía de Judy la ha enviado al aeropuerto a recoger a un cliente muy importante. Se trata del Sr. Moreau, que llega en el vuelo de París.

Judy: Sr. Moreau? Encantada de saludarle. Soy Judy Gardner de CEEI. He venido a recogerle para llevarle a la oficina.

Moreau: *(Le da la mano)* ¿Qué tal está usted? Muy amable por venir a buscarme.

Judy: ¿Tiene usted ya todo su equipaje?

Moreau: Sí. Sólo traigo este maletín.

Judy: Vamos, entonces. Tengo el coche aparcado fuera. ¿Qué tal el vuelo, Sr. Moreau?

Moreau: Muy bien. Estupendo. ... Disculpe, ¿ha dicho usted que se apellida Garland?

Judy: *(Riéndose)* Oh, no. Gardner. ¡No es la primera vez que me confunden con alguien famoso! Me apellido Gardner, y mi nombre es Judy. Trabajo para el Sr. Steinbeck.

Moreau: Ah, ya veo. *(Entran en el coche).*

Judy: Esta es su primera visita, me han dicho, ¿no?

Moreau: Sí, efectivamente. He estado tres o cuatro veces en Toronto, pero nunca aquí. Y es una pena, porque creo que hay muchas cosas que visitar.

Judy: Bueno, es lo que pasa con los viajes de trabajo. Todo son prisas y no hay tiempo para uno mismo.

Moreau: La verdad es que mi hija me había encargado un CD que acaba de salir con una recopilación de canciones de los Beatles – pero no voy a poder llevárselo.

Judy: No sé... Son sólo las tres y la reunión comienza a las cinco. ¿Quiere que le acompañe en un momento? De camino a la oficina, pasamos por delante de unos grandes almacenes.

Moreau: ¿De verdad hay tiempo? Le estaría muy agradecido, señorita Garland – digo... Gardner.

Judy: Sí. De verdad. Además, a esta hora hay poco tráfico.

Moreau: Se lo agradezco sinceramente: mi hija se pondrá muy contenta.

Judy: ¡Pero esto sólo se puede hacer a las tres de la tarde! Más tarde es imposible, por el tráfico.

Moreau: Vaya, entonces ¡igual que en París!

ACTIVITIES

1. True or False?

1. Monsieur Moreau is surprised that Judy's surname is Garland.
2. Judy has come to the airport to meet Monsieur Moreau and take him to the office.
3. This is Toronto Airport.
4. Monsieur Moreau regrets not having come to this city before.
5. When she says, "I don't know," Judy means she is calculating whether they have time to buy the CD.
6. They will have to wait until 3 p.m. to buy the CD.

2. Text Reconstruction
Put these boxes into a logical order:

| 1 | Oh, how do you do? It's very kind of you to pick me up. |

| 2 | Monsieur Moreau? Very pleased to meet you. I'm Judy Gardner. I've come to take you to the office. |

| 3 | Then let's go. |

| 4 | Do you have all your baggage with you? |

| 5 | Yes, all I have is this little case. |

ACTIVITIES

3. Find the phrase that...

1. **Expresa** un saludo cordial.
2. **Pregunta** por el equipaje.
3. **Describe** qué suele pasar en los viajes de negocios.
4. **Agradece** el favor de parte de su hija.
5. **Indica** qué hora es en ese momento.

4. Grammar Practice

Interrogative Phrases. Complete these questions by choosing a suitable verb from those offered to insert at the beginning, where you see this symbol ◆. Some sentences are from earlier dialogs.

WOULD   MAY   DO   DID   IS   CAN   DO   CAN

1. ◆ you have all your baggage with you?
2. ◆ you say your name was Garland?
3. ◆ you like to stop and look for it?
4. ◆ there anything else?
5. ◆ I help you?
6. ◆ I see some identification, please?
7. ◆ you have the other driver's details?
8. ◆ you manage a few minutes just after lunch, and get some ideas over a coffee?

15. AT THE HAIRDRESSER'S

Situation: Rose comes into a hairdressing salon and goes to the young woman at the counter.

Rose: Good morning. I want my hair dyed and styled, please.

Receptionist: Just a minute, while I make a note. What's your name, please?

Rose: Rose Miller. *(The receptionist notes it in a book).* Are there many people before me?

Receptionist: There *(closes the book).* Only two, ma'am. If you'll take a seat, you'll be attended to quite soon.

Rose: Thank you.

Hairdresser: It's your turn, ma'am. What would you like?

Rose: To have it dyed blonde and styled.

Hairdresser: Good. Please sit down here. Now let's see... Your hair is dark, and you've got quite a lot of gray hairs. If we dye it blonde straightaway, it won't have a good overall color and I don't think you'll like it. Let's see. *(She searches through the photos in an album).* What about this? In this photo the hair is dyed the same color as the eyebrows, and it's highlighted one tone lighter. That's what gives it this effect. Would you like it done this way? Bear in mind that it'll take a little longer.

Rose: That doesn't matter. I'm in no hurry. That's just the way I want it to look. Do it like the photo, please.

Hairdresser: I'm sure you'll like it. *(Three hours later).* Now, how do you want it styled, ma'am?

Rose: Curled, please, with the ends turned out. And no parting.

Hairdresser: Right. *(Twenty minutes later Rose's hair is done).* There you are. *(She holds up a mirror so that Rose can see the effect from behind).* How does it look?

Rose: Oh, that's lovely. *(Getting up).* How much is it?

Hairdresser: 42 euros, please.

Rose: Do you take VISA cards?

Hairdresser: Of course... Would you sign here, please? Here's your receipt, ma'am. And thank you for your custom.

Rose: Thank you. Goodbye.

15. EN LA PELUQUERIA

Situación: Rose entra en una peluquería y se dirige a la empleada que está en el mostrador.

Rose: Buenos días. Quiero teñirme y peinar.

Empleada: Espere, que le tomo nota. ¿Cuál es su nombre, por favor?

Rose: Rose Miller. *(La empleada lo apunta en una libreta).* ¿Tengo muchas personas delante?

Empleada: Ya está *(cierra la libreta)*. Solamente dos. Puede tomar asiento y la atenderán enseguida.

Rose: Gracias.

Peluquera: Le toca a usted, señora. ¿Qué se va a hacer?

Rose: Teñirme de rubio y peinarme.

Peluquera: Muy bien. Tome asiento, por favor. Déjeme ver.... Su pelo es castaño, y tiene usted bastantes canas. Si le pongo directamente rubio, no le va a quedar el color uniforme, y no le va a gustar. Vamos a ver. *(Busca entre las fotos de un álbum).* ¿Qué le parece? Esta modelo lleva un tinte del mismo color que las cejas, y encima, mechas de un tono más claro. Así se logra el efecto que ve. ¿Le parece que se lo haga? Tenga en cuenta que va a tardar un poco más.

Rose: No importa. No tengo prisa. Así es exactamente como lo quiero. Hágamelo igual que la foto.

Peluquera: Ya verá qué bien le queda. *(Pasan tres horas).* ¿Cómo quiere que la peine, señora?

Rose: Rizado, por favor. Con las puntas hacia arriba. Y no me haga raya.

Peluquera: Muy bien. *(Al cabo de 20 minutos, Rose está lista).* Ya está. Mire. *(Sostiene un espejo para que Rose se vea por detrás)* ¿Qué le parece?

Rose: Sí, está muy bien. *(Se levanta para irse).* ¿Qué le debo?

Peluquera: 42 euros, por favor.

Rose: ¿Admiten ustedes tarjetas VISA?

Peluquera: Sí, por supuesto... Firme aquí, por favor. Tenga el justificante. Y gracias por su visita.

Rose: Gracias. Adiós.

ACTIVITIES

---

1. True or False?

1. Rose goes to the hairdresser's to have her hair cut.
2. The receptionist assures Rose that she will not have to wait long.
3. Rose's hair is dark gray in color.
4. The hairstyle Rose chooses involves dyeing her eyebrows.
5. It takes three hours to style her hair.
6. Rose is delighted with the result.

2. What would you say in these situations?

1. Rose entra en una peluquería para teñirse y peinarse. ¿Qué le dirá a la peluquera?

   a) I want my hair dyed and styled, please.
   b) Do you color hair here?
   c) I want my hair cut and styled, please.

2. La peluquera te enseña una foto en la que la modelo lleva precisamente el peinado que te gusta.

   a) I don't like this girl. The style doesn't suit her.
   b) Yes, I like it, but I don't want my hair dyed the same color.
   c) That's just the way I want it to look.

3. La peluquera va a tardar al menos tres horas, y te lo hace saber, por si no lo tenías previsto. No te importa el tiempo porque no tienes prisa.

   a) How long will it take?
   b) I'm in no hurry.
   c) I have a lot of things to do. So, hurry up, please.

ACTIVITIES

3. Find the phrase that...

1. **Avisa** sobre el principal inconveniente: el tiempo que lleva realizar el peinado.
2. **Emplea** la peluquera para hacer saber a Rose que ya le toca.
3. **Dice** la razón por la que la peluquera desaconseja a Rose darse tinte rubio sobre el pelo que lleva ahora.
4. **Usa** la peluquera para preguntarle a Rose cómo quiere que la peine.
5. **Resume** las instrucciones que le da Rose a la peluquera sobre el peinado que quiere.

4. Grammar Practice

Personal Pronouns and Possessive Adjectives and Pronouns. Say these sentences aloud to include the missing pronoun or adjective. Some are taken from earlier dialogs. The number is parenthesis tells you how many times to use that word.

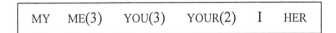

| MY | ME(3) | YOU(3) | YOUR(2) | I | HER |

1. I want ◆ hair dyed and styled, please.
2. What's ◆ name, please.
3. Are there many people before ◆?
4. Do ◆ take VISA cards?
5. Thank ◆ for ◆ custom.
6. It's very kind of ◆ to pick ◆ up.
7. My daughter asked ◆ to get ◆ a CD that's just come out.
8. Can ◆ help you?

16. ARRIVAL IN NEW YORK

Situation: Paul and Connie have just left J.F. Kennedy Airport to find a cab to their hotel.

Paul: There's a taxi coming now. Get some dollars ready, dear, and we'll see if we can avoid having to change a large bill.

Connie: How much do you think it'll cost?

Paul: I really don't know, but I imagine it'll be much the same as in London. ... Taxi! ... The Grand Hotel, please.

Driver: That your baggage? I'll put it in the trunk. *(On the way)* Your first time here?

Paul: No, but it's some while since we were last here.

Driver: Say, are you Britishers, by any chance?

Paul: Yes, from London.

Driver: I knew a guy from London once. Looked a bit like you, too – fairish and kind of lanky. Blue eyes, too, you know.

Paul: Oh, yes. I know. *(Starts talking to Connie to discourage the taxi driver from further comparisons).*

Driver: Well, here we are: the Grand. *(Gets their luggage out).* That's eleven bucks, please.

Connie: Bucks?

Paul: Dollars, dear! *(To the driver).* Keep the change, will you? Goodbye.

(In the hotel, they go to the counter. The receptionist greets them).

Recep.: Good morning. Can I help you?

Paul: Good morning. We have a room reserved – a double room, under the name of Paul Symmonds.

Recep.: *(Checking)* That is so. Your room number is four-three-four. ... Would you kindly sign here, please, Mr Symmonds? Here's the key. You're on the fourth floor; the elevators are over there. Enjoy your stay in New York!

Both: Thank you.

16. LLEGADA A NUEVA YORK

Situación: Paul y Connie acaban de llegar a Nueva York y están buscando un taxi.

Paul: Mira, ahí viene un taxi. Vete preparando algunos dólares para no tener que cambiar un billete grande.

Connie: ¿Cuánto crees que puede costar?

Paul: En realidad no lo sé, pero supongo que será más o menos como en Londres. ... ¡Taxi! ... Al Grand Hotel, por favor.

Taxista: ¿Es ése su equipaje? Lo pondré en el maletero. *(De camino)* ¿Es la primera vez que vienen?

Paul: No, pero hace tiempo que no veníamos.

Taxista: Oiga, ¿son ustedes ingleses por casualidad?

Paul: Sí; de Londres.

Taxista: Yo conocí una vez a un tipo que era de Londres. Tenía el aspecto parecido al suyo – muy rubio y delgaducho. Ojos azules, también, ya sabe.

Paul: Sí, ya lo sé. *(Se pone a hablar con Connie para que el taxista no siga con las comparaciones).*

Taxista: Aquí estamos. Este es el Grand Hotel. *(Saca el equipaje)*. Son 11 pavos.

Connie: ¿Pavos?

Paul: Dólares, cariño. *(Al taxista)* Tenga. Quédese con el cambio. Adiós.

(En el hotel, se acercan al mostrador de recepción. La recepcionista les saluda).

Recep.: Buenos días. ¿En qué puedo ayudarles?

Paul: Buenos días. Tenemos una habitación doble reservada a nombre de Paul Symmonds.

Recep.: *(Lo comprueba)*. Sí, efectivamente. Su habitación es la 434. ... Firme aquí, Mr Symmonds, por favor. Tenga, la llave. Su habitación está en el cuarto piso; los ascensores están allí. ¡Feliz estancia en Nueva York!

Ambos: Gracias.

ACTIVITIES

1. True or False?

1. Paul and Connie want to avoid paying much in the taxi.
2. They don't have to handle their baggage again.
3. Paul enjoys talking to the driver.
4. Paul says he knows the Londoner the driver is describing.
5. Paul tips the driver on arrival.
6. The hotel receptionist confirms their booking.

2. Text Reconstruction
Put these boxes into a logical order:

1	How much do you think it'll cost?

2	I really don't know, but I imagine it'll be much the same as in London. ... Taxi! ... The Grand Hotel, please.

3	There's a taxi coming now.

4	That your baggage? I'll put it in the trunk. *(On the way)* Your first time here?

5	No, but it's some while since we were last here.

ACTIVITIES

3. Find the phrase that...

1. **Sugiere** preocupación por tener que cambiar un billete grande en un taxi.
2. **Dice** qué hace el taxista con el equipaje.
3. **Presupone** la procedencia de Paul y Connie.
4. **Indica** que han llegado ya al hotel.
5. **Da** la bienvenida a los visitantes.

4. Grammar Practice

Pronouns. In this exercise, in which some examples come from earlier dialogs, you have to replace the nouns, in **bold letters**, *by their corresponding pronoun form.*

1. I'll put **your baggage** in the trunk.
2. Get **some dollars** ready.
3. Paul starts talking to **Connie.**
4. Keep **the change**, will you?
5. The receptionist greets **Paul and Connie.**
6. **Paul and Connie** are in New York.
7. **Monsieur Moreau** is arriving on the Paris flight.
8. **The hairdresser** searches through the photos in an album.
9. I work for **Mr Steinbeck**.
10. I'll check up with **Susan** this evening and give you a call.
11. Have you brought **your policy**?
12. Is **Shirley** in, please?

17. AT THE DOCTOR'S OFFICE

Situation: John hasn't been feeling well for some days, so he telephones for an appointment with a local doctor. The receptionist answers the telephone.

Recep.: Dr. Wilson's office. Good morning.

John: Good morning. Can you give me an appointment to see the doctor, please?

Recep.: Yes, of course... How about tomorrow morning at nine?

John: All right. Put me down for nine a.m., please.

Recep.: Your name, please?

John: John Addams – with a double D.

Recep.: Right, Mr Addams. Dr. Wilson will see you at nine tomorrow.

(John is shown into the doctor's room)

Doctor: Good morning, Mr Addams. Please take a seat and tell me what's wrong.

John: I haven't felt right for several days, doctor. My head aches, I cough quite a lot, and last night I was feverish and shivering a lot in bed.

Doctor: H'm. Let's have a look at you. Take your shirt off and sit on the couch, please. Take a deep breath... Again... Now once more... Right. Now your throat. Say: aaah... Right; you can get dressed again. Well, Mr Addams, it's nothing serious, but besides a very heavy cold, you've got the beginning of flu. You'll have to take these tablets – one every eight hours, for seven days. Here's the prescription. The best thing for you would be not to leave the house for the next two or three days, too. Tell me, what sort of work do you do?

John: It's an ordinary office job. But we're especially busy at present and I wouldn't like to stay away too long.

Doctor: Well,... Make sure to wrap up well when you go out and avoid drafts. We don't want your cold to get any worse!

John: Thanks, doctor. I'll follow your advice. *(They shake hands).*

Doctor: So long as you do, you'll be back to normal in no time. Goodbye, Mr Addams.

John: Goodbye, doctor.

17. EN LA CONSULTA DEL MEDICO

Situación: John se encuentra mal desde hace unos días. Llama a la consulta del médico para pedir cita. Contesta la recepcionista.

Recep.: Consulta del Dr. Wilson. Buenos días.

John: Buenos días. Llamo para pedir cita con el doctor.

Recep.: Sí, vamos a ver... ¿Le parece bien mañana a las 9?

John: De acuerdo. Tómeme nota, por favor.

Recep.: ¿Me da su nombre?

John: John Addams – se escribe con doble "d."

Recep.: Muy bien, Sr. Addams. Tiene cita para mañana por la mañana a las nueve con el doctor Wilson.

(John entra en la consulta del médico)

Doctor: Buenos días, señor Addams. Tome asiento, por favor, y dígame lo que le ocurre.

John: Doctor, hace días que no me encuentro bien. Me duele la cabeza; toso bastante, y anoche tenía fiebre y escalofríos.

Doctor: H'm. Déjeme que le examine. Siéntase en la camilla y descúbrase el pecho. Respire hondo... Otra vez... Una vez más... Bien. Ahora, la garganta. Diga: "aaah." Bien, puede vestirse. Sr. Addams, no es serio, pero tiene usted un catarro muy fuerte y principio de gripe. Va a tomarse estos comprimidos. Uno cada 8 horas, durante 7 días. Tenga la receta. Lo ideal sería que no saliera de casa durante dos o tres días. Dígame, ¿en qué trabaja usted?

John: En una empresa. Pero ahora tenemos mucho trabajo y no me gustaría faltar.

Doctor: Bueno, ... Procure abrigarse bien cuando salga y evite las corrientes de aire. ¡No quiero que empeore ese catarro!

John: Gracias, doctor. Seguiré su consejo. *(Se estrechan la mano)*.

Doctor: Ya verá cómo mejorará pronto. Adiós, Sr. Addams.

John: Adiós, doctor.

ACTIVITIES

1. True or False?

1. Although he is unwell, John does not go to the doctor's at once.
2. The receptionist gives him an appointment for the day after tomorrow.
3. The tablets the doctor prescribes are to be taken every eight hours.
4. The doctor also advises him to stay indoors.
5. Deciding to follow the doctor's advice, John will not leave the house for a long time.
6. The doctor's diagnosis includes two ailments.

2. What would you say in these situations?

1. Hace días que te encuentras mal con síntomas de catarro y gripe. Llamas por teléfono a la consulta del médico y pides cita.

   a) I'm not feeling well. I need a doctor urgently.
   b) Can you give me an appointment to see the doctor, please?
   c) I'm coming. Please tell the doctor to wait for me.

2. Has llamado a la consulta del médico para pedir cita. La recepcionista te dice una hora, las nueve de la mañana. A ti te parece bien. ¿Qué dices?

   a) OK. Put me down for nine a.m., please.
   b) Could the doctor come to my house, please?
   c) OK. Put me down for eight a.m., please.

3. Ahora, supongamos que tu interlocutor es el Sr. Addams. En la conversación te ha dado un consejo. Quieres agradecérselo y decirle que lo seguirás.

   a) Please tell me, what's your opinion?
   b) Thanks, Mr Addams, I'll follow your advice.
   c) Thank you, but I can take care of myself.

ACTIVITIES

3. Find the phrase that...

1. **Emplea** John para explicar al doctor los síntomas que tiene.
2. **Invita** a pasar y sentarse.
3. **Usa** el doctor al examinar el pecho y la garganta de un paciente.
4. **Afirma** de que la dolencia de John no es grave.
5. **Resume** el consejo del médico para cuando John vaya a salir de casa.

4. Grammar Practice.

A. Phrasal Verbs. Reread the dialog and then say these sentences, inserting a particle from the box where you see the symbol ◆, to complete each Phrasal Verb.

```
AWAY   BACK   DOWN   OFF   UP
```

1. Put me ◆ for nine a.m., please.
2. Take your shirt ◆ and sit on the couch, please.
3. We're especially busy at present and I wouldn't like to stay ◆ from the office too long.
4. Make sure to wrap ◆ well when you go out.
5. You'll be ◆ to normal in no time.

B. Cloze Test. From the following paragraph, eight words have been omitted. Find them in the box and replace them where you see the symbol ◆.

```
BESIDES   BEGINNING   IT'S   TABLETS   HERE'S
         HOURS   COLD   HAVE
```

Well, Mr Addams, ◆ nothing serious, but ◆ a very heavy ◆, you've got the ◆ of flu. You'll ◆ to take these ◆ —one every eight ◆ for seven days. ◆ the prescription.

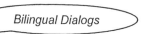

18. HAVING WORK DONE IN THE HOUSE

Situation: Jenny and her husband have decided to have some work done in their home. The contractor, a man named Burns, calls to note down what is to be done and take measurements.

Jenny: (Opening the door) Yes?

Burns: James Burns, ma'am. I'm the contractor. You asked me to call.

Jenny: Oh, yes. Come in, Mr Burns... Well, as my husband told you, we want to modernize the bathroom - and have the house repainted. Come this way, will you. This is the bathroom. *(Burns takes out a notebook).* What we want is a thorough change: new piping, a new electrical installation, and of course more modern equipment. This bathroom hasn't been touched since we moved in twelve years ago, you see.

Burns: Do you have any particular model of equipment in mind?

Jenny: Well, we'd like you to give us some ideas. ... I guess you have catalogs?

Burns: Naturally. I'll send you a selection to choose from.

Jenny: Good. Now the other thing was the repainting. We want the whole house done. But please take a look at this room first – the kids' room. You see that wall? They've scrawled all over it. Will it have to be scraped off first?

Burns: Oh, no. Don't worry. It can just be painted over.

Jenny: I want plastic paint – you know: the kind you can wash down.

Burns: No problem. That's the kind we get asked for most.

Jenny: Now how long will all this take?

Burns: It can be done within a month at the outside: bathroom and painting – the lot.

Jenny: Uh-huh. That suits us fine. And when can you give us an estimate?

Burns: Let me see. I'll have it mailed to you the day after tomorrow, along with the catalogs, so you'll get it on Friday. And if you agree, we can start work *(looking at the calendar)* in three weeks' time.

Jenny: So, we can count on having it finished about two months from now, can we? Well, as soon as we get the estimate, we'll think it over and give you an answer. *(Opens the door).*

Burns: OK, ma'am. I'll be waiting to hear from you. *(Shakes her hand as he goes out).* I can assure you you'll be more than satisfied. Goodbye.

Jenny: Goodbye.

18. OBREROS EN CASA

Situación: Jenny y su marido han decidido hacer reforma en la casa. Llaman a la puerta. Es Burns, el contratista, que llega para tomar nota y medidas de lo que desean.

Jenny: *(Abre la puerta)* ¿Sí?

Burns: James Burns, señora. Soy el contratista. Me han llamado ustedes.

Jenny: Ah, sí. Pase, Sr. Burns. Bueno, como le dijo mi marido, queremos reformar el baño y pintar la casa. Pase por aquí. Este es el baño. *(Burns saca una libreta).* Lo queremos reformar al completo: las cañerías, nuevas, una nueva instalación eléctrica y, desde luego, sanitarios más modernos. Sabe... este baño no se ha arreglado desde que vinimos a vivir hace doce años.

Burns: ¿Tienen pensado algún modelo de sanitarios?

Jenny: Queríamos que usted nos diera algunas ideas. ... Supongo que tienen catálogos, ¿no?

Burns: Naturalmente. Le enviaré unos cuántos para que puedan elegir.

Jenny: Vale. Ahora lo siguiente es la pintura. Queremos pintar toda la casa. Pero primero quiero que vea esta pared... Es la habitación de los niños. ¿Ve la pared? Está toda pintada. ¿Va a tener que rasparla?

Burns: No. No se preocupe. Desaparece al dar la nueva pintura.

Jenny: Quiero que ponga pintura plástica lavable.

Burns: Sí, desde luego. Es lo que más nos piden.

Jenny: ¿Cuánto tardan ustedes?

Burns: En un mes, como mucho, lo tiene todo hecho: la reforma del baño y la pintura.

Jenny: ¡Ah, ja! Está bien. ¿Cuándo nos puede usted pasar el presupuesto?

Burns: Vamos a ver. Se lo pongo en el correo pasado mañana junto con los catálogos, de modo, que el viernes que viene ya lo tendrá. Y si están de acuerdo, podemos empezar la obra *(mira el calendario)* dentro de 3 semanas.

Jenny: Bueno. Así que podemos contar con que esté todo terminado dentro de dos meses, ¿no? *(Abre la puerta).*

Burns: Exacto, eso es, señora. Pues quedamos así, espero su llamada. *(Le estrecha la mano).* Ya verá qué bien le va a quedar. Adiós.

Jenny: Adiós.

ACTIVITIES

1. True or False?

1. Jenny and Burns want to redecorate their home.
2. On arrival at the house, the contractor has no idea what he will have to do.
3. The bathroom has been the same for twelve years.
4. Burns will have to scrape the bedroom wall before painting it.
5. Washable paint will be used on the children's room.
6. Jenny and her husband will not decide on the job until they have seen how much it will cost them.

2. Text Reconstruction
Reorder these boxes to make a sensible dialog:

1	Oh, no. Don't worry. It can just be painted over.

2	Now the other thing was the repainting. We want the whole house done. But please take a look at this room first – the kid's room. You see that wall? They've scrawled all over it. Will it have to be scraped off first?

3	No problem. That's the kind we get asked for most.

4	I want plastic paint – you know: the kind you can wash down.

ACTIVITIES

3. Find the phrase that...

1. **Indica** el motivo por el que ha venido Burns.
2. **Describe** en qué consiste la reforma del baño.
3. **Sugiere** que los niños han estropeado la pared del dormitorio.
4. **Asegura** que la reforma quedará muy bien.
5. **Dice** la clase de pintura que se empleará para pintar la pared del dormitorio de los niños.

4. Grammar Practice

Interrogative Words. Instead of the symbol ♦, *select the right interrogative word from the box for each question. Some questions are from earlier dialogs. The number in parenthesis tells you how often to use that word.*

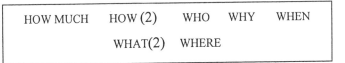

```
HOW MUCH   HOW (2)   WHO   WHY   WHEN

           WHAT(2)   WHERE
```

1. ♦ long will all this take?
2. ♦ can you give us an estimate?
3. ♦ about tomorrow morning at nine?
4. ♦ do you think it'll cost?
5. ♦ is your name, please?
6. ♦ shall I sign?
7. ♦ have you come to New York?
8. ♦ could inform me?
9. ♦ do you want to talk about?

19. AT A CAR DEALER'S

Situation: Leslie wants to buy a new car. He and his friend George go to a Chrysler dealer and walk along among the models on show. A salesman comes up to them.

Salesman: Good afternoon, gentlemen. Can I be of any help?

Leslie: We're just having a look at this four-door model. What kind of engine does it have?

Salesman: It's equipped with a standard 2.4-liter, 150 horsepower engine.

Leslie: What's the gas mileage?

Salesman: 21-mpg in the city and 29-mpg on the highway.

Leslie: And, what's included in the base price?

Salesman: Well,... power steering, air-conditioning, power central locking system, power windows, and airbags for driver and front passenger. And we offer the floor mats for free.

George: *(Looking at the price shown on the windshield).* Are you prepared to pay this much, Les? It isn't a cheap model!

Leslie: I reckon we could afford it. And Judy would love this upholstery! *(To the salesman).* Is the price fully inclusive?

Salesman: All our prices include registration as well as taxes, sir.

Leslie: I see. Then another question: Can I trade in my old car for this model?

Salesman: Sure. We would assess the trade-in value of your car and deduct that amount from the price.

George: Uh-huh. And what are the optional extras?

Salesman: Well... Here, gentlemen, please take a catalog, in which the optional extras are specified *(gives them one each)* and my card. My name is Swaine.

Leslie: Well, I'd like my wife to see it, too, before making a decision.

Salesman: Naturally. We are open from nine till one and from three to eight, including Saturdays. We'll be very pleased to see you again whenever you care to call in, sir. *(They shake hands).* Goodbye.

Both: Goodbye.

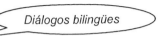

19. EN UN CONCESIONARIO DE COCHES

Situación: Leslie quiere comprarse un coche nuevo. El y su amigo George van a un concesionario de Chrysler. Están paseando entre los modelos expuestos. Se acerca un vendedor.

Vendedor: Buenas tardes, señores. ¿Les puedo ayudar en algo?

Leslie: Estábamos mirando este modelo de cuatro puertas. ¿Qué motor tiene?

Vendedor: Motor gasolina 2.4 litros y 150 CV de potencia.

Leslie: ¿Y cuánto consume?

Vendedor: 21 millas por galón en ciudad y 29 millas por galón en carretera.

Leslie: ¿Qué equipamiento presenta de serie?

Vendedor: Lleva de serie: dirección asistida, aire acondicionado, cierre centralizado, elevalunas eléctrico, y airbags del conductor y del acompañante. Y se regalan las alfombrillas.

George: *(Mirando el precio que está puesto en el parabrisas).* ¿Has visto el precio, Les? ¡No es precisamente barato!

Leslie: Ya, pero, hombre, lo podría pagar. Además, ¡a Judy le va a encantar la tapicería! *(Se dirige al vendedor).* En el precio, ¿está todo incluido?

Vendedor: Todos nuestros precios incluyen impuestos y matriculación.

Leslie: Ya. Me gustaría hacerle otra pregunta: ¿me tasarían el coche viejo y lo aceptarían como parte del pago?

Vendedor: Desde luego que sí. Le haríamos una tasación y se lo descontaríamos del precio total.

George: Ah, ya. ¿Y cuáles son las opciones de equipamiento adicional?

Vendedor: Bien... Tengan, señores, llévense este folleto del coche, donde se especifican los extras *(entrega uno a cada uno),* y mi tarjeta. Yo soy Swaine.

Leslie: Me gustaría enseñárselo a mi mujer también, antes de decidir.

Vendedor: Por supuesto. Nuestro horario es de 9 a 1 y de 3 a 8, inclusive los sábados. Estaremos encantados de atenderles las veces que quieran venir. *(Extiende la mano para estrechársela a los dos).* Adiós.

Ambos: Adiós.

ACTIVITIES

1. True or False?

1. Leslie takes George to buy a new car.
2. They are interested in a car with four doors.
3. The salesman tries to sell them the dearest model.
4. Leslie's old car will be part of the deal.
5. The dealer's does not close at midday.
6. Leslie evidently thinks he and his wife should decide on the car together.

2. What would you say in these situations?

1. Estás viendo el coche que quieres comprar. Una de las cuestiones más importantes es el gasto de gasolina. ¿Cómo lo preguntas?

   a) What's the gas mileage?
   b) Is the maintenance on this car very expensive?
   c) I can't afford a car that uses a lot of gas.

2. La mayoría de concesionarios compran el coche viejo del cliente a cambio de uno nuevo. Quieres saber si éste es el caso para el coche que te interesa.

   a) Can I trade in my old car for this model?
   b) Could you buy my old car? You would do me a favor.
   c) Please keep my old car. It's horrible!

3. Al comprar un coche, quieres saber entre qué extras puedes elegir.

   a) What else can you offer me?
   b) What are the optional extras?
   c) My wife likes leather upholstery. Could you include this in the purchase price?

ACTIVITIES

3. Find the phrase that...

1. **Usa** Leslie para preguntar cuánto gasta el coche de combustible.
2. **Sugiere** que se trata de un modelo caro.
3. **Resume** lo que el concesionario haría con el coche viejo de Leslie.
4. **Indica** que el vendedor les entrega un catálogo a cada uno.
5. **Informa** sobre el horario del concesionario.

4. Grammar Practice

Compound Nouns. Many nouns in English are compound. That is, they consist of two successive nouns, sometimes joined and sometimes separate, where the first acts as an adjective and the second is the real noun. In this exercise you have to pair them from the two columns, in the order given, to make familiar compounds. Some are from earlier dialogs.

1. horsepower	a) model
2. base	b) engine
3. power	c) mats
4. gas	d) mileage
5. floor	e) bags
6. four-door	f) job
7. air	g) table
8. office	h) room
9. kitchen	i) price
10. bath	j) windows

20. RADIO INTERVIEW

Situation: Professor José Merino is being interviewed on the radio.

Interviewer: In our program today we have Professor José Merino, author of countless books on learning English. Good afternoon, Professor Merino.

Professor: Good afternoon to you and all your listeners.

Interviewer: Professor, why is it that Spanish-speaking students so often complain that, in spite of having studied English for such a long time, they have so much difficulty in understanding the spoken language?

Professor: You've asked me a significant question. Well, to begin with, the English language contains groups of consonants that are hard for a Spanish-speaker to distinguish and harder still to pronounce. Yet they determine much of the sense of the utterance and the meaning of many of its words. On the other hand, vowels in English hardly ever coincide with those in Spanish. And on top of all this is the problem of intonation, which counts so much.

Interviewer: Does intonation play a part in making ourselves understood, then?

Professor: Certainly. How many of us have said something that we know is correctly pronounced, yet the natives do not understand? It's our intonation that is faulty. This, then, gives us the answer to your question – we don't understand because we are hearing sounds that we do not expect. In the teaching of English, it would be desirable to include special courses on phonetics.

Interviewer: And a final question: why is it so hard to learn a foreign language?

Professor: It is hard because in order to really learn it, one has to *think* in it, which requires study and dedication... plenty of reading, and of course, plenty of practice in speaking it. That's the only way of mastering it.

Interviewer: That is all we have for today. Professor Merino, many thanks for your presence here this afternoon and for this useful contribution.

Professor: Many thanks to you. It has been a pleasure.

Diálogos bilingües

20. ENTREVISTA EN LA RADIO

Situación: El profesor José Merino es entrevistado en la radio.

Entrevist.: Hoy en nuestro programa, tenemos al profesor José Merino, autor de innumerables libros para aprender inglés. Buenas tardes, profesor Merino.

Profesor: Buenas tardes, a usted y a todos los oyentes.

Entrevist.: Profesor, ¿por qué se quejan los estudiantes de habla española de que, a pesar de haber estado estudiando inglés durante mucho tiempo, tienen dificultad en entender el inglés hablado?

Profesor: Me hace usted una pregunta muy interesante. Bien, por una parte, en inglés hablado se dan grupos de consonantes de difícil captación y pronunciación para un hispano hablante. Sin embargo, de ellos depende el sentido de la frase y el significado de muchas palabras. Y por otra, las vocales inglesas no suenan igual que las vocales españolas. A esto debemos añadir el factor de la entonación, que tiene tanta importancia.

Entrevist.: Entonces, ¿esto significa que la entonación juega un papel importante para ser entendido?

Profesor: Por supuesto. ¿Cuántas veces un estudiante dice una frase correctamente pronunciada que un nativo no parecen entender? Es debido a la entonación, que no es correcta. Esto, entonces, nos da la respuesta a la pregunta: No entendemos porque oímos sonidos que no esperamos, y perdemos el significado. En la enseñanza del inglés, sería necesario impartir cursos especiales de fonética inglesa.

Entrevist.: Y ahora una última cuestión: ¿Por qué resulta tan difícil llegar a dominar un idioma?

Profesor: Es difícil porque para ello hay que *pensar* en él, y esto requiere estudio y dedicación,... leer mucho,... y, por supuesto, practicar mucho el lenguaje hablado. Así es cómo se logra llegar a dominarlo.

Entrevist.: Pues esto ha sido todo por hoy. Profesor Merino, gracias por acompañarnos esta tarde, y aclararnos algunas ideas.

Profesor: Muchas gracias a ustedes. Ha sido un placer.

ACTIVITIES

1. True or False?

1. Professor Merino has written countless books on learning English.
2. The interview takes place shortly before lunch.
3. A long study of English does not mean that Spanish-speakers necessarily understand the language when they hear it spoken.
4. Pronouncing English correctly does not mean that the speaker will always be understood.
5. The professor says that mastering English depends entirely on practice.
6. The professor's recommendation is phonetics courses to help students understand sound differences.

2. Text Reconstruction
Construct a meaningful dialog by reordering these boxes:

1	Professor, why is it so hard to learn a foreign language?

2	It is hard because in order to really learn it, one has to *think* in it, which requires study and dedication... plenty of reading, and of course, plenty of practice in speaking it.

3	In our program today we have Professor José Merino, author of countless books on learning English. Good afternoon, Professor Merino.

4	Good afternoon to you and all your listeners.

5	That is all we have for today. Professor Merino, many thanks for your presence here this afternoon and for this useful contribution.

ACTIVITIES

3. Find the phrase that...

1. **Indica** que la conversación tiene lugar en la radio.
2. **Resume** la principal queja de los hispano-hablantes respecto del idioma inglés.
3. **Asegura** la importancia de la entonación para ser entendido.
4. **Da las claves** para llegar a dominar un idioma.
5. **Usa** el entrevistador para despedir el programa.

4. Grammar Practice

Cloze Test. From this paragraph, every sixth word has been removed and put into the box. Put them all back into their correct places (♦). "Of" will be needed twice.

TO	OF(2)	IS	SPEAKING	REALLY
	THINK	AND		

— Why is it so hard ♦ learn a foreign language?
— It ♦ hard because in order to ♦ learn it, one has to ♦ in it, which requires study ♦ dedication... plenty of reading, and ♦ course plenty of practice in ♦ it. That's the only way ♦ mastering it.

TEAMWORK

Esta sección contiene una serie de actividades para trabajo en equipo, bien en clase, o entre compañeros.

Dialog 1: A CHAT BETWEEN FRIENDS AFTER WORK.

Open Questions
1. How long has Mark been waiting for Charlie?
2. What do they order to eat?
3. What do they order to drink?
4. How's Charlie doing at work?
5. What does Mark tell his friend?
6. How many rooms does Mark's new house have?
7. Are they going to move to their new house?
8. Who pays?

Conversation Topics
1. What dishes are the most popular?
2. What drinks are the most popular?
3. Fast food or homemade food.

Role-play
1. Replay this dialog with your partners.
2. Now suppose that when going to pay, nobody has enough money. How does the dialog change?

Dialog 2: AT THE INSURANCE COMPANY.

Open Questions
1. Where has Simon gone?
2. What does the clerk ask Simon for first?
3. What happened during the accident?
4. What damage does Simon's car have?
5. What damage do you suppose the other vehicle might have?
6. Was anyone injured?
7. Was it a minor or a major accident?

8. If you have you had a car accident, did you follow the same procedure as Simon?

Conversation Topics
1. Traffic regulations. Do you think that people obey them?
2. Give your opinion about how a person's behavior changes when he is driving.
3. Describe the main causes of car accidents.

Role-play
1. Replay this dialog using the same words.
2. Suppose that somebody was injured in the accident. Make up the dialog.

Dialog 3: IN THE HOME.

Open Questions
1. What does Mary have to do every day?
2. And what is the special chore for today?
3. Which chores does Rose say are not necessary?
4. Why is the plumber coming?
5. Where does Rose have to go?
6. Where did Rose leave the money for the plumber?
7. What should Mary do if there is a telephone call?
8. When the plumber arrives, who's in the house?

Conversation Topics
1. Housework.
2. Do you think chores should be shared among the members of the family? Give your opinion.
3. Buying groceries in a supermarket.

Role-play
1. Replay the same dialog.

TEAMWORK

2. Now let's suppose that Mary has gone to sleep while watching television. She awakes when Rose arrives. She hasn't bought the bread or heard from the plumber. Adapt the dialog accordingly.

Dialog 4: AT A CAR REPAIR SHOP.

Open Questions
1. Why has Michael gone to the car repair shop?
2. What needs to be done to the car?
3. Does Michael think that the price is fair?
4. What is the freebie this month?
5. Why can't Michael leave the car until the next morning?
6. What's the mechanic's proposal?
7. What time does the car repair shop close?
8. Do you have a car? If so, how often do you take it to the car repair shop?

Conversation Topics
1. Give your opinion on the following: is it better to take the car to the dealer's repair shop or to any car repair shop?
2. Give your opinion on the benefits of keeping your car in good condition.
3. In your opinion, are there any car models that need less maintenance?

Role-play
1. Replay the same dialog.
2. Suppose that when picking up the car, Michael realizes that a tire is flat, and he can't use the car. Adapt the dialog accordingly.

Dialog 5: A TELEPHONE CONVERSATION BETWEEN TWO WOMEN.

Open Questions
1. What relationship does Rose have with Shirley?
2. Who answers the telephone?
3. What is the favor that Rose asks of Shirley?
4. Who is the costume for?
5. What costume accessories are missing?

TEAMWORK

6. What makes them laugh?
7. What does Shirley advise Rose to do?
8. What time will they meet to pick up the costume?

Conversation Topics
1. Activities children do in school.
2. Talk about parent participation in school activities.
3. Common parent concerns.

Role-play
1. Replay this dialog using the same words.
2. Let's suppose it's the girls, Laura and Lucy, and not their mothers, that are talking on the telephone. Make up the possible dialog that could take place.

Dialog 6: MANAGEMENT MEETING.

Open Questions
1. How many people are present at the meeting?
2. How many men and how many women are there?
3. What are they talking about?
4. What is the reason why the company intends to employ two more salespeople?
5. When would the new salespeople be hired?
6. When is the new product supposed to be launched?
7. What is the main factor that will determine the launch of the product?
8. What does this mean: "an estimate of monthly sales"?

Conversation Topics
1. The development of a business.
2. Professional relationships between the managers of a company: teamwork, co-ordination, etc.
3. Do you think it's possible for the managers of the same company to be friends outside the office?

TEAMWORK

Role-play
1. Replay this dialog using the original words.
2. Let's suppose that a representative of an advertising agency also attends the meeting and explains how they could launch the product. Adapt the dialog.

Dialog 7: LOOKING FOR A FLAT.

Open Questions
1. Where exactly is the flat that Beverly wants to buy?
2. Describe the flat: how many rooms does it have?
3. How did Beverly find out that the flat was on sale?
4. Is the parking space under the building included in the price?
5. What floor is the flat on?
6. Do you think that the owner is willing to lower the price?
7. Why is the owner selling the flat?
8. What time are they meeting the next day?

Conversation Topics
1. Types of homes.
2. Home prices.
3. Steps you have to take when buying a flat.

Role-play
1. Replay this dialog with a partner.
2. Now let's suppose that instead of calling on the telephone, Beverly goes to a real estate agency and asks for the same flat. Invent a conversation.

Dialog 8: AN EVENING WITH FRIENDS.

Open Questions
1. How many people are participating in this dialog?
2. What is the relationship between them?
3. What are they eating?

TEAMWORK

4. What are they drinking?
5. What are they talking about?
6. What are the reasons why Sally would forgive her husband if he had an affair?
7. Why doesn't Jane agree with Sally?
8. What does Alex propose to toast?

Conversation Topics
1. Give your opinion on the following: are we really honest when giving our opinion among friends?
2. Talk about jealousy and unfaithfulness.
3. Discuss how to prepare a house party for your friends.

Role-play
1. Replay this dialog with your partners.
2. Adapt the dialog introducing the following change: Suddenly Sally realizes that Jane is the person who has been having an affair with her husband Ted.

Dialog 9: LOOKING FOR AN APARTMENT TO RENT.

Open Questions
1. Where did Eddie find the advertisement for the apartment for rent?
2. When Eddie calls, who answers the telephone?
3. Where is the apartment?
4. How many bedrooms does the apartment have?
5. What type of kitchen does it have?
6. What's included in the rent?
7. What's not included in the rent?
8. What is Eddie's occupation?

Conversation Topics
1. Advantages and disadvantages of living in the city center versus the country.
2. Possible conflicts between the landlord and the tenant.

3. Which is preferable? To rent or to own an apartment?

Role-play
1. Replay this dialog using the original words.
2. When the landlord comes to the apartment, he realizes that the tenant has remodeled it completely. Invent the conversation.

Dialog 10: A CONVERSATION BETWEEN TWO SISTERS IN A CAR.

Open Questions
1. What is the relationship between Ann and Betty?
2. Where are Ann and Betty going?
3. Where is the furniture store?
4. What are they talking about?
5. What problems do their friends Bill and Molly have?
6. What do they think about their friends' problems?
7. How do they the find the store that they are looking for?
8. Who puts the gas in their car?

Conversation Topics
1. Give your opinion about the factors that may cause a divorce.
2. Talk about a lawyer's role in the divorce process.
3. Give your opinion about a psychologist's or a consultant's role in mediating a divorce situation.

Role-play
1. Replay this dialog.
2. Adapt the dialog introducing the following change: Betty, who is driving, gets lost.

Dialog 11: SHOPPING.

Open Questions
1. Why did Brian and Rose go to the department store?
2. Where is the men's department?

TEAMWORK

---

3. Do the pants need to be tailored?
4. What type of tailoring do the pants need?
5. Did Brian try on the pants?
6. What does Rose comment when Brian asks how the pants look?
7. When can Brian pick up the pants?
8. How does Brian pay for the pants?

Conversation Topics
1. Fashion.
2. Different fabrics for clothes.
3. Types of suits for every occasion.

Role-play
1. Replay this dialog.
2. Now it is Rose who needs an evening dress for a party. Invent the dialog that may take place.

Dialog 12: A CONVERSATION IN THE OFFICE.

Open Questions
1. Who is in the office and who enters?
2. Why has Jean gone to the office so early?
3. Why is Sylvia all wet?
4. What does Jean propose to Sylvia?
5. Why are Jean and Sylvia going to get together?
6. Where are they going to meet?
7. What time are they going to meet?
8. Has Arthur come yet?

Conversation Topics
1. Do you think that employees gossip a lot?
2. Give your opinion about having a break in the middle of the workday.
3. Give your opinion whether you would rather have your own business or be employed by a company.

TEAMWORK

Role-play
1. Replay this dialog.
2. Now let's suppose that Jean and Betty are criticizing their boss, Roger. Suddenly he enters the room. Invent the dialog that follows.

Dialog 13: AT THE BANK.

Open Questions
1. Why has John gone to the bank?
2. What does the clerk ask for before he can proceed with the transaction?
3. What's the mistake the bank has made?
4. What must the clerk do with John's savings book?
5. Why does John need a form?
6. What information must be filled out on the form?
7. Why does John want to talk to the manager?
8. Who informs customers in a bank how to invest money?

Conversation Topics
1. Which is best? Having your money in bank accounts, buying stocks, investing in a home, keeping your money at home or ... spending it?
2. Which is better? Paying by credit card or cash?
3. Which is better? Sharing accounts with your spouse or keeping them separate?

Role-play
1. Replay this dialog.
2. Now let's suppose that the bank clerk lives near the golf club. He has seen John at the club many times. Therefore he doesn't want to reimburse John for the golf club subscription. Adapt the dialog accordingly.

Dialog 14: PICKING UP A CUSTOMER AT THE AIRPORT.

Open Questions
1. Who is Monsieur Moreau?
2. Where does Judy work and who for?

3. Why does Monsieur Moreau get confused by Judy's name?
4. How are they going to the office?
5. What has Monsieur Moreau's daughter asked him to buy?
6. Is there enough time to buy it for her?
7. Where's the department store where they can buy the CD?
8. How many conversation topics has Judy thought of on the way to the office?

Conversation Topics
1. Agree or disagree: The customer is always right.
2. Business traveling. Is it glamorous or is it difficult? Give your opinion.
3. Talk about popular music groups around the world.

Role-play
1. Replay this dialog.
2. Replay this dialog introducing the following change: It's five p.m. and the meeting is about to start. Judy and Monsieur Moreau are still in the car because there's a terrible traffic jam. Monsieur Moreau is beginning to get nervous. Make up the dialog.

Dialog 15: AT THE HAIRDRESSER'S.

Open Questions
1. What is Rose's intention in going to the hairdresser's?
2. Why does the hairdresser say Rose may not like the result?
3. Does Rose follow the hairdresser's advice?
4. How much time does Rose spend at the hairdresser's?
5. How much does it cost?
6. What color is Rose's hair naturally?
7. What color does Rose want her hair to be dyed?
8. How does Rose want her hair styled?

Conversation Topics
1. Describe beauty treatments for men and for women.

TEAMWORK

2. Do you think it's better for older people to cover their gray hair or leave it natural?
3. Types of hairstyles for men or women depending on the situation.

Role-play
1. Replay this dialog, taking into account whether your partner is a man or a woman.
2. Let's suppose that the hairdresser has made a mistake and Rose's hair is now red. What dialog would follow?

Dialog 16: ARRIVAL IN NEW YORK.

Open Questions
1. What city are Paul and Connie visiting?
2. Where are they from?
3. What is the taxi driver's description of the British?
4. Why does Paul want Connie to have some change ready?
5. What is the fare?
6. What's the name of the hotel they are staying at?
7. How long are they going to stay in New York?
8. What's Paul's last name?

Conversation Topics
1. Give your opinion on why people talk to taxi drivers.
2. Have you been abroad? Talk about your travels.
3. Recommendations a travel agency gives to a client before going on a trip.

Role-play
1. Replay this dialog.
2. Paul and Connie realize that the driver has passed their destination twice. Adapt the dialog.

TEAMWORK

Dialog 17: AT THE DOCTOR'S OFFICE.

Open Questions
1. Why does John call Dr. Wilson's office?
2. What time does the receptionist make the appointment for?
3. What symptoms does John have?
4. What's the diagnosis?
5. What does the doctor prescribe?
6. What's the doctor's advice?
7. Can John follow the doctor's advice?
8. What sort of work does John do?

Conversation Topics
1. Common diseases.
2. Give your opinion on people's fear of doctors and hospitals.
3. Public Health and Private Health.

Role-play
1. Replay this dialog.
2. Let's suppose that John has been taking another medication on his own, with no result. When the doctor gives him a prescription, John feels obliged to tell the doctor. Adapt the conversation.

Dialog 18: HAVING WORK DONE IN THE HOUSE.

Open Questions
1. What remodeling is Jenny planning for her house?
2. Why does Burns take out a notebook?
3. What does she want to do to the bathroom?
4. Why does she want to change the piping?
5. What has happened to the wall in the kids' room?
6. What kind of paint are they going to use to paint the house?
7. How long will it take?
8. Why is Burns sending a catalog to Jenny?

TEAMWORK

Conversation Topics
1. Give your opinion about which is preferable: remodeling a house or selling it and buying a new one.
2. Talk about the attitude the owner must have with the contractors.
3. When a house needs remodeling or repairs, which is preferable: to call a contractor or to try to do things by oneself?

Role-play
1. Replay this dialog.
2. Let's suppose that Jenny and Burns get annoyed with each other. The workmen have gone and left the house a complete mess. Now Jenny has two problems: explaining to her husband what happened and finding another contractor. Invent the dialog.

Dialog 19: AT A CAR DEALER'S.

Open Questions
1. What's the car make that Leslie likes?
2. What type of engine does the car have?
3. What's included in the base model?
4. What's the gas mileage?
5. What is George's opinion of the price?
6. Does the price include any extras?
7. Why doesn't Leslie decide there and then?
8. What are the opening hours?

Conversation Topics
1. Car makes and types.
2. Reasons why people buy cars.
3. Talk about what people value most in a car.

Role-play
1. Replay this dialog.
2. The car dealer is trying to show John a luxury car, but what John really needs is a van for work. Create the dialog that follows.

TEAMWORK

Dialog 20: RADIO INTERVIEW.

Open Questions
1. Who is Professor Merino?
2. What is today's program about?
3. How many questions does the radio interviewer ask?
4. Why is it so difficult for a Spanish-speaking student to understand spoken English?
5. Is it true that English vowels hardly ever coincide with those in Spanish?
6. What is the key to mastering a foreign language?
7. Why does Professor Merino recommend attending courses on English phonetics?
8. Why does Professor Merino recommend plenty of reading?

Conversation Topics
1. Give your opinion: what information must an interviewer have about the person who's going to be interviewed?
2. Discuss the different methods of learning or teaching English.
3. The importance of the English language in the world.

Role-play
1. Replay this dialog using the original words.
2. Now let's suppose that Professor Merino gave only very brief answers to the questions. What would the interviewer do in this situation?

ANSWER KEY

En esta sección se ofrecen las soluciones a las actividades.

Dialog 1: A CHAT BETWEEN FRIENDS AFTER WORK.

1. 1 – false. 2 – true. 3 – false. 4 – true. 5 – false. 6 – true.
2. 1. a) Hi, Mark. Here I am. Been waiting long?
   2. b) Well, Charlie, what's new? How's the job going?
   3. c) I'll check up with Susan this evening and give you a call.
3. 1. Are you ready to order now, sir?
   2. How far is your new house from there, Mark?
   3. I'm getting on pretty well now. I've been given a special project to work on, and it's coming along nicely.
   4. It's rather small, as I said – only two bedrooms.
   5. Oh, and you can just put that wallet back.
4. A. a small house; a cheeseburger; the nearest village; fruit trees; a special project; day-to-day shopping; ten minutes.
   B. 1) I'm getting on pretty well now.
   2) The project is coming along nicely.
   3) We drove through it a week or two ago.
   4) I'll check it up with Susan this evening.
   5) You can put that wallet back.

Dialog 2: AT THE INSURANCE COMPANY.

1. 1 – false. 2 – false. 3 – true. 4 – true. 5 – false. 6 – false.
2. El orden es: 3 – 2 – 1 – 4 – 5.
3. 1. I'm fully covered.
   2. Had the light changed against you, by any chance?
   3. Well, I was coming out of Bernard Street and turning left onto Moon Street. A van, which was stopped at the traffic lights in the opposite direction, suddenly started, ran the red light and crashed into my right-hand door.
   4. And I take it you were going fairly slowly.
   5. All you have to do now is take it to any of the workshops that do repairs for us.

ANSWER KEY

4. 1. I'll just locate you on the computer.
2. Please give me the details of the accident.
3. A van was stopped at the traffic lights.
4. The van crashed into my right-hand door.
5. There's a big dent in my door.
6. Now, take the car to any of the workshops that do repairs for us.
7. We drove through Woodlake a week or two ago.
8. How far is your new house from there?
9. The house is ample for weekends.

Dialog 3: IN THE HOME.

1. 1 – true. 2 – true. 3 – true. 4 – false. 5 – false. 6 – true.
2. 1. c) Could you slip out and get me some bread this morning? We're right out.
2. b) Uh-oh, how forgetful of me! I nearly forgot: the plumber's coming later on.
3. b) I really must be off to work.
3. 1. Apart from that, just sweep up and mop the floor as usual, please.
2. There's some small change in the Chinese pot on the mantelpiece.
3. If anyone calls by telephone, take a message, will you, and get the number so that I can call back.
4. Well, now I really must be off to work.
5. Come in, please. It's this way. It's the sink here; it's clogged, you see.
4. A. 1. Mop the floor.
2. Don't bother about the windows.
3. Do water the plants if you have time, will you?
4. Take the number so that I can call back.
5. Get the message.
6. Come in, please.
7. Let's have a look.
B. 1. What do you want me to do today?
2. It is ironing day today.
3. Do not bother about the windows.

ANSWER KEY

4. We are right out.
5. He said he would be coming this morning.
6. I have only got to go out for the bread.
7. After that I will be in all morning.
8. If you need anything, I am in the kitchen.

Dialog 4: AT A CAR REPAIR SHOP.

1. 1 – false. 2 – true. 3 – false. 4 – true. 5 – true. 6 – true.
2. El orden es: 2 – 4 – 1 – 3 – 5.
3. 1. I'd like you to give this car a thorough check-up.
   2. We're doing this for the whole of January. Each check-up this month includes a wash, inside and outside.
   3. I've got to be at the airport at ten to pick someone up.
   4. What about payment? Shall I settle up now or when I come for the car?
   5. Are the keys in the car?

4. A. 1. Is there something I can do for you?
   2. How long would it take?
   3. I can't afford to leave it too long.
   4. What about payment? Shall I settle up now or when I come for the car?
   5. Could you slip out and get me some bread this morning?
   B. 1. We have a special offer all this month, if you are interested.
   2. When can we come and see it?
   3. Don't bother about the windows until it stops raining.
   4. Do water the plants if you have time, will you?
   5. I wasn't too happy at first, but now I've been given a special project to work on.

Dialog 5: A TELEPHONE CONVERSATION BETWEEN TWO WOMEN.

1. 1 – false. 2 – true. 3 – false. 4 – false. 5 – true. 6 – false.
2. 1. a) Who's calling, please?

ANSWER KEY

2. c) Well, how can we arrange it? Shall I come round for it – at about eight, say?
   3. b) See you then, Robert. Bye.
3. 1. It's a Cinderella costume.
   2. But what I don't have is the hair ribbon and the shoes.
   3. You know how cold it is in the school theater!
   4. No, they did at first, but I made her wear several petticoats over them, and in the end the dress looked very cute.
   5. It's well worth filming. I thought it was superb last time.
4. A. 1. I didn't know who it was at first.
   2. I'm calling to ask a favor of you.
   3. I need a costume for Laura.
   4. Don't worry about the ribbon and the shoes.
   5. You know how cold it is in the school theater.
   B. 1. I'll just call her.
   2. See you then, Shirley. Bye.
   3. They won't be visible anyway.
   4. It certainly is!
   5. In the end the dress looked very cute.

Dialog 6: MANAGEMENT MEETING.

1. 1 – true. 2 – false. 3 – false. 4 – false. 5 – true. 6 – true.
2. El orden es: 1 – 3 – 4 – 2.
3. 1. The articles will have to be run off as they sell.
   2. You'll have to tell me exactly *when* you need them and what qualifications you want them to have.
   3. They'll need to be working with us two months before the product goes on the market if we're to have time enough to get them trained.
   4. The cost of the raw materials, the ongoing production costs, the salaries of these new employees, and the marketing bill and the trading expenses that all this will entail.
   5. They would have to begin work in February, so that we could launch the product in April.

ANSWER KEY

---

4. That's all very well, but there's something important to bear in mind: that we can't just start manufacturing a run of 100,000 units. The articles will have to be run off as they sell. So I'd need an estimate of monthly sales. And also over a whole year.

Dialog 7: LOOKING FOR A FLAT.

1. 1 – true. 2 – false. 3 – false. 4 – true. 5 – false. 6 – true.
2. 1. c) Good afternoon. I'm calling to ask about the flat you're advertising in The Times.
    2. b) Well, first, where is it situated exactly?
    3. a) Would tomorrow be convenient? How about five p.m.?
3. 1. The price is a bit higher than we can really afford. Is it negotiable, by any chance?
    2. Who should I expect?
    3. I'm only selling it because my office is being transferred elsewhere and shall have to find a new home there.
    4. The ad mentions a space in the car park under the building. That goes with the flat.
    5. The flat is on the fifth floor, overlooking the park, not the main road.
4. A. 1. How can I help you?
      2. Where is it situated exactly?
      3. What about parking?
      4. Who should I expect?
      5. Why don't you come along and see it?
    B. 1. How can I help you?
      2. My husband must be able to put his car away safely.
      3. I think I know where that is.
      4. It sounds right for us.
      5. My name is Jenkins.

Dialog 8: AN EVENING WITH FRIENDS.

1. 1 – false. 2 – true. 3 – true. 4 – false. 5 – true. 6 – true.
2. El orden es: 3 – 1 – 4 – 2 – 5.

ANSWER KEY

3. 1. Thanks to her, your marriage, your home... it's all at risk, not to mention your bank account. We all know about legal costs!
2. But to my mind maybe one little slip in a marriage lifetime can be overlooked – so long as it doesn't happen again!
3. Yes, *I* do. Just a drop, please.
4. You're really some cook, Sally!
5. This is something well worth celebrating!

4. 1. This is something well worth celebrating!
2. Not to mention your bank account.
3. What's to stop you having a smack and tickle now?
4. It means there's nothing to hold you back now!
5. My husband has too much to do to waste his time on some girl who's only out for promotion.
6. The kitchen's clean, and don't bother about the windows until it stops raining.
7. Now I really must be off to work.
8. How come you offer a car wash free?

Dialog 9: LOOKING FOR AN APARTMENT TO RENT.

1. 1 – true. 2 – false. 3 – true. 4 – false. 5 – false. 6 – true.
2. 1. a) Do you know what that means?
2. c) Forgive my asking, but do you earn a fixed salary?
3. b) How big is it? I mean, what does it consist of?
3. 1. And the kitchen is totally electric.
2. It couldn't be more central.
3. The address is in the advertisement: Shaftesbury Avenue, number 1.
4. The kitchen is marked off from the living room by a counter.
5. Does the rent include heating and so on?
4. A. 1. Are you interested in renting it?
2. Do you know what that means?
3. Is that so?
4. Does the rent include heating?
5. Do you earn a fixed salary?
6. Would you like to see the apartment?

ANSWER KEY

B. 1. I'm calling about the apartment you're advertising.
2. The address is in the advertisement.
3. The kitchen is marked off from the living room by a counter.
4. You would have to pay for the water you use.
5. Apartments of this type aren't easy to find.

Dialog 10: A CONVERSATION BETWEEN TWO SISTERS IN A CAR.

1. 1 – false. 2 – false. 3 – true. 4 – false. 5 – true. 6 – true.
2. El orden es: 3 – 1 – 4 – 2 – 5.
3. 1. Number ten, Wharfedale Street.
   2. She told me that they're always quarreling; but it's been getting worse lately and she can't put up with it any longer.
   3. Apparently, yes. At least, that's what he says. I wouldn't trust him, you know.
   4. But I do wish they'd gone to a marriage guidance specialist long before it came to this. It might have saved the marriage.
   5. Thank you very much indeed.
4. 1. Do you know where that is?
   2. I only know where Commercial Road is.
   3. Turn off at the next corner.
   4. But what does Bill say about it?
   5. I'm going to pull up at that service station.
   6. I'll go and ask that old gentleman over there.
   7. I'm calling about the apartment you're advertising.
   8. This is something well worth celebrating!

Dialog 11: SHOPPING.

1. 1 – false. 2 – true. 3 – true. 4 – false. 5 – true. 6 – false.
2. 1. c) Excuse me. The men's section – which floor is it?
   2. a) Cash or credit card?
   3. b) When will they be ready?
3. 1. I'd like to try them on.
   2. We don't charge for altering our own articles.

ANSWER KEY

---

   3. Cash or credit card?
   4. On Thursday, sir – any time in the morning.
   5. And please don't forget to bring this ticket with you.
4. A. 1. The men's section, which floor is it?
     2. It's a free service, sir.
     3. I'll come along and measure them for length.
     4. I should think that half an inch will do.
     5. Please don't forget to bring this ticket with you.
 B. 1. We have to go up to the second floor.
     2. These pants look rather long to me.
     3. Are they comfortable? Yes, they are comfortable enough.
     4. When will they be ready ?
     5. Oh, yes. That's just right.

Dialog 12: A CONVERSATION IN THE OFFICE.

1. 1 – false. 2 – false. 3 – true. 4 – true. 5 – true. 6 – false.
2. El orden es: 2 – 4 – 3 – 1 – 5.
3. 1. Hello, Jean! You here already? It's early for you!
   2. I only hope it clears up before lunch; I've come without an umbrella.
   3. How about you and me getting together to talk about the meeting?
   4. It's the advertising agency's estimate. Goodness! What they charge!
   5. Give it to Arthur. When Roger's traveling, he authorizes all that kind of thing. Then file it under "Conventions."
4. A. 1. She takes her raincoat off and shakes it well before hanging it up.
     2. I only hope it clears up before lunch.
     3. This fax came in for you about five minutes ago.
     4. I heard him moving about in his office a few minutes ago, so he's in.
 B. 1. Is it raining?
     2. It started the very moment I got off the bus.
     3. I've come without an umbrella.
     4. This fax came in for you about five minutes ago.
     5. What do you want to talk about?
     6. I'm asking you because Roger's not here.
     7. I heard him moving about in his office.

ANSWER KEY

Dialog 13: AT THE BANK.

1. 1 – false. 2 – false. 3 – true. 4 – true. 5 – false. 6 – false.
2. 1. c) First, would you please bring this up to date?
    2. b) May I see some identification, please?
    3. b) Would you sign here, please?
3. 1. I want to pay this check into another account I have with you. Where are the forms, please?
    2. This copy is for you.
    3. Yes, you're quite right: I'm afraid it's our mistake. I'm very sorry indeed.
    4. I'll cancel that debit at once.
    5. I don't think he's busy at the moment and I'm sure he'll be only too pleased to help you.
4. A. 1. I'm very sorry indeed.
    2. It'll save you time.
    3. That's quite correct.
    4. There's a mistake.
    5. I'll check that for you.
    6. You're quite right.
  B. 1. I don't think the manager is busy at the moment.
    2. I want to pay this check into another account I have with you.
    3. I don't belong to a golf club.
    4. I'll check that for you.
    5. I'd like to know a little more about one of the services you offer.

Dialog 14: PICKING UP A CUSTOMER AT THE AIRPORT.

1. 1 – false. 2 – true. 3 – false. 4 – true. 5 – true. 6 – false.
2. El orden es: 2 – 1 – 4 – 5 – 3.
3. 1. Very pleased to meet you.
    2. Do you have all your baggage with you?
    3. Well, business trips are like that, aren't they? It's all go, go, go, and no time for yourself.
    4. It's very good of you: my daughter will be so pleased.

ANSWER KEY

---

    5. It's only three o'clock and your meeting doesn't start until five.

4. 1. Do you have all your baggage with you?
    2. Did you say your name was Garland?
    3. Would you like to stop and look for it?
    4. Is there anything else?
    5. Can I help you?
    6. May I see some identification, please?
    7. Do you have the other driver's details?
    8. Can you manage a few minutes just after lunch, and get some ideas over a coffee?

Dialog 15: AT THE HAIRDRESSER'S.

1. 1 – false. 2 – true. 3 – false. 4 – false. 5 – false. 6 – true.
2. 1. a) I want my hair dyed and styled, please.
    2. c) That's just the way I want it to look.
    3. b) I'm in no hurry.
3. 1. Bear in mind that it'll take a little longer.
    2. It's your turn, ma'am.
    3. If we dye it blonde straightaway, it won't have a good overall color and I don't think you'll like it.
    4. How do you want it styled, ma'am?
    5. Curled, please, with the ends turned out. And no parting.
4. 1. I want my hair dyed and styled, please.
    2. What's your name, please.
    3. Are there many people before me?
    4. Do you take VISA cards?
    5. Thank you for your custom.
    6. It's very kind of you to pick me up.
    7. My daughter asked me to get her a CD that's just come out.
    8. Can I help you?

Dialog 16: ARRIVAL IN NEW YORK.

1. 1 – false. 2 – true. 3 – false. 4 – false. 5 – true. 6 – true.

ANSWER KEY

---

2. El orden es: 3 – 1 – 2 – 4 – 5

3. 1. Get some dollars ready, dear, and we'll see if we can avoid having to change a large bill.
   2. I'll put it in the trunk.
   3. Say, are you Britishers, by any chance?
   4. Well, here we are: the Grand.
   5. Enjoy your stay in New York!

4. 1. I'll put it in the trunk.
   2. Get them ready.
   3. Paul starts talking to her.
   4. Keep it, will you?
   5. The receptionist greets them.
   6. They are in New York.
   7. He is arriving on the Paris flight.
   8. She searches through the photos in an album.
   9. I work for him.
   10. I'll check up with her this evening and give you a call.
   11. Have you brought it?
   12. Is she in, please?

Dialog 17: AT THE DOCTOR'S OFFICE.

1. 1 – true. 2 – false. 3 – true. 4 – true. 5 – false. 6 – true.

2. 1. b) Can you give me an appointment to see the doctor, please?
   2. a) OK. Put me down for nine a.m., please.
   3. b) Thanks, Mr Addams, I'll follow your advice.

3. 1. I haven't felt right for several days, doctor. My head aches, I cough quite a lot, and last night I was feverish and shivering a lot in bed.
   2. Good morning, Mr Addams. Please take a seat and tell me what's wrong.
   3. Take a deep breath... Again... Now once more... Right. Now your throat. Say: aaah... Right.
   4. Well, Mr Addams, it's nothing serious.
   5. Make sure to wrap up well when you go out and avoid drafts.

4. A. 1. Put me down for nine a.m., please.

2. Take your shirt off and sit on the couch, please.
3. We're especially busy at present and I wouldn't like to stay away from the office too long.
4. Make sure to wrap up well when you go out.
5. You'll be back to normal in no time.
B. Well, Mr Addams, it's nothing serious, but besides a very heavy cold, you've got the beginning of flu. You'll have to take these tablets – one every eight hours, for seven days. Here's the prescription.

Dialog 18: HAVING WORK DONE IN THE HOUSE.

1. 1 – false. 2 – false. 3 – true. 4 – false. 5 – true. 6 – true.
2. El orden es: 2 – 1 – 4 – 3.
3. 1. James Burns, ma'am. I'm the contractor. You asked me to call.
   2. What we want is a thorough change: new piping, a new electrical installation, and of course more modern equipment.
   3. But please take a look at this room first – the kids' room. You see that wall? They've scrawled all over it.
   4. I can assure you you'll be more than satisfied.
   5. I want plastic paint – you know: the kind you can wash down.
4. 1. How long will all this take?
   2. When can you give us an estimate?
   3. How about tomorrow morning at nine?
   4. How much do you think it'll cost?
   5. What is your name, please?
   6. Where shall I sign?
   7. Why have you come to New York?
   8. Who could inform me?
   9. What do you want to talk about?

Dialog 19: AT A CAR DEALER'S.

1. 1 – false. 2 – true. 3 – false. 4 – true. 5 – false. 6 – true.
2. 1. a) What's the gas mileage?
   2. a) Can I trade in my old car for this model?

ANSWER KEY

---

   3. b) What are the optional extras?

3. 1. What's the gas mileage?

   2. Are you prepared to pay this much, Les? It isn't a cheap model!

   3. We would evaluate your existing car and deduct that amount from the price.

   4. Here, gentlemen, please take a catalog.

   5. We are open from nine till one and from three to eight, including Saturdays.

4. 1 – b = horsepower engine.

   2 – i = base price.

   3 – j = power windows.

   4 – d = gas mileage.

   5 – c = floor mats.

   6 – a = four-door model.

   7 – e = airbags.

   8 – f = office job.

   9 – g = kitchen table.

  10 – h = bathroom.

Dialog 20: RADIO INTERVIEW.

1. 1 – true. 2 – false. 3 – true. 4 – true. 5 – false. 6 – true.

2. El orden es: 3 – 4 – 1 – 2 – 5.

3. 1. Good afternoon to you and all your listeners.

   2. Why is it that Spanish-speaking students so often complain that, in spite of having studied English for such a long time, they have so much difficulty in understanding the spoken language?

   3. Certainly. How many of us have said something that we know is correctly pronounced, yet the natives do not understand? It's our intonation that is faulty.

   4. It is hard because in order to really learn it, one has to *think* in it, which requires study and dedication... plenty of reading, and of course, plenty of practice in speaking it. That's the only way of mastering it.

ANSWER KEY

5. That is all we have for today. Professor Merino, many thanks for your presence here this afternoon and for this useful contribution.

4. — Why is it so hard to learn a foreign language?
   — It is hard because in order to really learn it, one has to *think* in it, which requires study and dedication... plenty of reading, and of course, plenty of practice in speaking it. That's the only way of mastering it.

CATALOGO GRATUITO

Solicite de forma gratuita nuestro catálogo completo de *Libros Didácticos Complementarios – Resource Material* escribiendo a la siguiente dirección, o llamando al teléfono que se indica.

Anglo-Didáctica Publishing
c/ Santiago de Compostela, 16 – bajo B
28034 Madrid, España
Tel y Fax: (34) 91 378 01 88